The American Woman's Garden

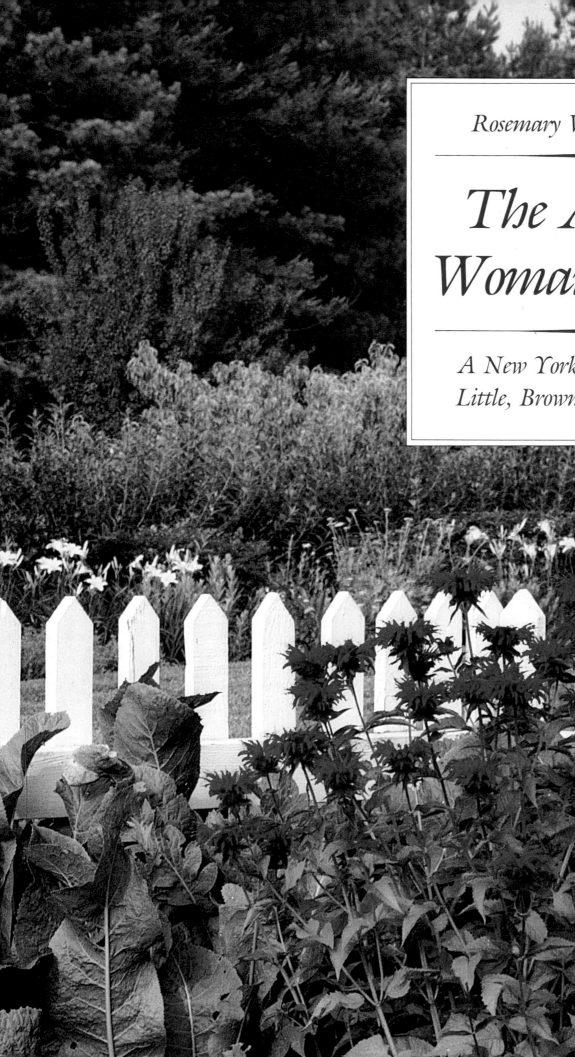

Rosemary Verey · Ellen Samuels

The American Woman's Garden

A New York Graphic Society Book
Little, Brown & Company · Boston

To my husband, David Verey,
who shared my journeys to the United States

R. V.

To my children, Evelyn, John, Ainlay, and Peter

E. S.

First Edition

Printed in Italy

Library of Congress Cataloging in Publication Data

Verey, Rosemary.
   The American woman's garden.

   "A New York Graphic Society book."
   1. Gardens — United States. 2. Women gardeners —
United States. 3. Landscape gardening — United States.
I. Samuels, Ellen. II. Title.
SB466.U6V47 1984   712'.6'0973   84-12257
ISBN 0-8212-1580-9

Title page illustration: The garden of Jane Symmes, Madison, Georgia.

Preface

THERE ARE MOMENTS when an idea captivates you and you wish to pursue it at once. This happened for me when Ellen Samuels suggested that we might produce a book with the help of American women gardeners in a format similar to *The Englishwoman's Garden,* which Alvilde Lees-Milne and I had edited in 1979. It was not until the articles began to arrive on my desk in England that I realized quite how much I was going to learn about American gardens, and I was unprepared for the wealth of talent there is among its women gardeners. In these thirty articles the reader is led gently along by the gardeners, through old estate gardens, through city yards where every inch is used to advantage, through gardens that are a family heritage and others, just as lovingly nurtured, that are new yards around new houses.

During my trips to the United States, both before this book was envisaged and in preparation for it, I have been warmly and generously received. I am reminded of James Pope-Hennessy's statement that "the kindness of Americans is without question more general, more warming and unvarying than that of any other peoples. It is in the deepest sense a national characteristic." I can mention here only a few instances of the kindnesses I received, but the others will not be forgotten.

I was taken around the Brooklyn Botanic Garden in 1978 by Frederick McGourty, through the kind thought of Elizabeth Scholtz. It was the first American garden I had seen, and it remains a standard for me. On that first trip I also visited in Raleigh, North Carolina, with Ollie Adams, whose theme is the use of American indigenous perennial plants, perhaps in improved forms. Why not, I ask, bearing in mind that many of our best herbaceous perennials came from the United States?

Sally Lee and Kathie Pitney showed me some New Jersey gardens and I was especially attracted by the lovely mix of formal and informal planting at Pitney Farm, the home of the Pitney family since 1720. On another visit I at last saw the Philadelphia Flower Show, where I was much impressed with the efforts and ideas put forward by American women gardeners. Our Chelsea Flower Show is almost entirely professional, but in Philadelphia the amateurs make important contributions in flower arrangement, house-plant displays, and even topiary in pots to winter indoors. Ernesta Ballard was then, in 1980, serving her last year as show director, to be succeeded by Jane Pepper; these two women have filled one of the most influential horticultural positions in the United States. Another very active member of the Pennsylvania Horticultural Society is Kathy Buchanan, who showed me about the gardens of the Philadelphia area, impressive even in the wintry March weather.

Back in New York, Anne and Frank Cabot were full of advice and outstanding help, taking me to see the remarkable Wave Hill garden in the city and their own well-known garden and alpine nursery at Cold Spring.

Peggy Rockefeller introduced me to some of the gardens of Maine, and most especially was extremely generous with her time in showing me about her own extraordinary garden at Seal Harbor.

On the West Coast, a visit to Filoli was essential, and I was taken there by George and Olive Waters. George is editor of *Pacific Horticulture,* surely one of the best horticultural magazines in circulation today. Other friends have guided me to gardens in Virginia, Missouri, Texas, and South Carolina.

My knowledge of American gardens has been greatly augmented by reading. Elizabeth Hall, for many years librarian of the New York Horticultural Society, and Elisabeth B. MacDougall, librarian at Dumbarton Oaks, have shown me many of their treasures. Elizabeth Woodburn, with her bookshop in Hopewell, New Jersey, has been most helpful in tracing old American garden books for me.

To these people, and to all those who have helped to educate me concerning American gardens, through visits and reading, I say thank you.

However, without Ellen this book would not have happened. She has traveled around the country searching for the finest gardens cared for by women. She has been through every climate zone in the States, journeying many thousands of miles with a wonderful result. (To me back in England it is the extremes of climate and the consequent vast difference in growing conditions that has surprised me most.) I wish I had had the opportunity to visit all the gardens, and to meet all the owners so I could thank them personally for their wonderful contributions to this book. One day this may happen.

Since my first visit to the United States I have been a firm admirer of American gardens, their style and wealth of plants. But one thing always worries me: American visitors to England play down their own gardening achievements and murmur that they cannot do as well as we can here. This I have long known to be untrue, and now the contributors to this book have played into my hands; not only are they the creators and keepers of marvelous gardens of an infinite variety, but they have written about them with great knowledge, enthusiasm and charm. I thank them all.

Rosemary Verey   December 1983

*I*T IS ROSEMARY VEREY'S generous reception of American visitors to her garden at Barnsley House in the Cotswolds that has made this book possible. The garden is of such interest and artistry that, like Sissinghurst and Wisley, it is on the short list of essential stops for any horticultural expedition from across the Atlantic. And like those gardens it repays repeated visits over the seasons and years. Her laburnum walk is becoming as much a symbol of the romance of English gardening as the white garden at Sissinghurst.

When I began searching for gardens for this book, we wrote off to the most enthusiastic signers of Rosemary's visitors' book. The resulting encouragement, advice, and offers of assistance made it possible for me to see gardens in more than fifty cities and towns in less than a year. And in each city, if I did not run into someone who had actually been to Barnsley, I always met those who admired it through her books.

In this country, Rosemary and I were fortunate enough to have the advice and assistance of Mrs. Donald Straus, Mrs. Erastus Corning ii, and Charles Webster. Beth Straus, who has contributed so much to the gardens of the Museum of Modern Art and the New York Botanic Gardens, introduced me to gardeners from Santa Barbara to Stockbridge and made the Vereys' and my visit to Maine especially pleasant. Betty Corning, former president of the Garden Club of America and key member of its Rare Plant Group, was a constant source of encouragement and information. Chuck Webster, chairman of the New York Horticultural Society, was the kindest of advisors.

Eleanor Weller, who is compiling the Garden Club of America's library of slides of notable parks and gardens, which includes the superb collection of hand-colored lantern slides that the GCA commissioned in the twenties and thirties, was an encyclopedic source of information. So was William Lanier Hunt, honorary president of the Southern Garden History Society, who has been teaching and writing about gardens of that region for more than fifty years. George Waters, editor of Pacific Horticulture, was an indispensable guide to the gardens of the west coast.

So many were involved in the pursuit of the American woman's garden that there simply isn't space to list them all. About halfway through my travels I began to feel I could not pick up the phone again and ask another acquaintance or friend of a friend for assistance in finding gardens in her area. But I did, and my calls continued to receive the most helpful responses imaginable. I want to note, though, that without Joan Fleming in Houston, Wendy Powell in Kansas City, and Jean Woodhull in Dayton I might never have ventured to those cities and discovered their remarkable gardening traditions. Janie Pratt and her husband John, who took the pictures, made it possible for us to have a Carolina low-country plantation in the book. Janie is also working to restore the gardens of Richmond Plantation, now owned by the local Girl Scouts organization, and so preserve for the public this unique aspect of regional social and horticultural history. Gingy Coulter in Lake Forest, Helen Lewis Bixby in St. Louis, and Harriet Nevins in Tucson will find gardens they showed me in our next book.

Having my brother Jack Richards and his wife Karin living in London and my parents John and Leontine in San Francisco made my travels particularly pleasant. The hospitality of Ruth and Henry Morgenthau in Cambridge was especially appreciated during my frequent trips to Boston to work with the publisher. Fittingly enough, it is a quotation from Henry's aunt that ends the Epilogue.

I am most grateful to Marina Schinz, who was the first to help me understand the art of garden photography, for her photograph on the book's dust jacket.

Betty Childs, who has been creatively involved with the book from its earliest stages, has been the wisest and most sympathetic of editors.

It has been a joy to work with all the contributors. My sole regret is that one book can only hint at the richness of the American gardening scene.

Ellen Samuels   May 1984

Contents

Contents

An English View of the American Woman's Garden

ROSEMARY VEREY

THE WIVES OF THE SETTLERS from England in the early seventeenth century are among the first women gardeners we know about in North America. While their husbands worked in the fields, the women helped to keep themselves and their families alive by growing herbs and vegetables. In the ships sailing to the new land they had brought seeds, plants, and their precious herbals, but almost as important were the memories they brought of the gardens they had left behind: of English gardens, in simple style, laid out with formal beds for herbs and vegetables and scented plants such as rosemary, lavender, and pinks for their fragrant posies or "tussie mussies." But in the first years they had no time for the niceties of arranging their plants in carefully planned beds — the soil had to be cultivated, the seeds sown, the crop gathered and stored in good condition for next winter's food and the next season's sowing. Some years after the first settlement, John Winthrop wrote in his journal as his ship approached Boston after ten weeks at sea, "We had now fair sunshine weather and so pleasant a sweet Aire as did much refresh us, and there came a smell off the shore like the smell of a garden." The women had made a good beginning. In time the gardens became more ornamental and reminiscent of the formal Tudor and Stuart gardens back in England, with geometric beds, garden houses, and picket fences.

Today many American women have discovered that through their gardens they can satisfy their instinct for creating or maintaining something beautiful, in just the same way as their counterparts in England are doing. Gardening is a refuge from the hustle and hurry of our twentieth-century way of life. It offers a two-way bonus: satisfaction for those who garden, and joy for those who visit. In both our countries there are old gardens being cherished and new ones created. It is quite clear in the articles written by my compatriots for *The Englishwoman's Garden,* and now by American women for this book, that gardening is part of our way of life, and to some of us it is as important as eating and drinking.

I find it remarkable that so many historic gardens are being preserved on both sides of the Atlantic in spite of the difficulties of staff, upkeep, and inheritance duties. In Georgia, Alice Callaway cares for a garden with spectacular boxwood

The rock garden created by Eulalie Wagner at Lakewold, her home in Tacoma, Washington.

made by Sara Coleman Ferrell nearly a century and a half ago; in Santa Barbara, Medora Bass nurtures her father's Andalusian garden. Here in England, with exactly the same sentiments, Lady Salisbury keeps alive the two gardens that have been in her husband's family since John Tradescant traveled to America in the seventeenth century in search of plants. Our instincts are all the same.

My interest in American gardens dates back to the time I began collecting books on horticulture and, naturally, came upon literature about American gardens. Best of all, for me, was *Gardens of Colony and State,* compiled and edited for the Garden Club of America by Alice G. B. Lockwood in 1931 and 1934. The black-and-white photographs gave me a wonderful picture of the gardens of that time. Ann Leighton's *Early American Gardens* and *American Gardens in the 18th Century* gave me a fascinating insight into American garden history, early libraries and plants. So my appetite was whetted, and I found other valuable references on American gardens. *Historic Virginia Gardens* by Dorothy Hunt Williams is a record of the important preservations made by the Garden Club of Virginia and is of inestimable value. Louisa Farrand Wood, a niece of Beatrix Farrand, celebrated her eightieth birthday in 1983 by publishing her first book, entitled *Behind Those Garden Walls in Historic Savannah.* I would recommend it to any owner of a small garden wishing to make the most of her site. In complete contrast, for it is neither about history or formal gardens, is *A Southern Garden* by Elizabeth Lawrence, published in 1942. Mrs. Lawrence reveled in the poetry of the garden, and her writing about her garden in North Carolina is reminiscent of Vita Sackville-West or E. A. Bowles. She was a pioneer in the use of perennials, and her book is a treasury of plant associations. It is one you cannot put down.

These are favorites among the books that have contributed to my knowledge of American gardens. I selected them casually from my shelves, and now I find that they were all written by women.

During four trips to the United States, I have come to appreciate something of the accomplishments of American women gardeners. But I was especially pleased on a trip to the West Coast in 1981 to see a fine estate garden that is being beautifully maintained by the Filoli Center. Twenty-five miles south of San Francisco, Filoli was built early in this century by William Bowers Bourn II, on a site that reminded him of the beautiful countryside by the lakes of Killarney in Ireland. Its importance for gardeners dates from the time it was bought by Lurline and William Roth in 1937. Mrs. Roth, together with landscape designer Bella Worn, transformed the garden devised by Bruce Porter for William Bourn. Their original color and planning concept for the annual beds is still continued: pansies and violas in winter followed by petunias and pelargoniums in summer.

On the day of our visit I was impressed by the formality of the pool, with domes of tidy gray-leaved teucrium dominating each corner. The knot garden looked wonderful, with its carefully clipped threads emphasizing the traditional patterns of interlacing "overs and unders." But I was undoubtedly jealous of the speed with which the knot garden had taken on its well-established shape; in my Cotswold garden it has taken twice as many years to attain this effect.

The avenue of Irish yews, *Taxus baccata* 'Stricta', creates an imposing vista, and trees chosen for contrast of shape and color make a fine display, especially the two weeping elms, *Ulmus glabra* 'Camperdownii', the golden-leafed locust, *Gleditsia triacanthos* 'Sunburst', and bronze-red maples. Filoli is a peaceful oasis with a distant backdrop of hills and an immediate shelter of California live oaks estimated to be more than five hundred years old. The whole garden has an atmosphere of well-being and beauty, because of choice planting and high standard of upkeep. Visitors should remember gratefully the horticultural wisdom bestowed upon it by Lurline Roth, who gave the house and garden to the National Trust for Historic Preservation in 1975 in order that their beauty might be shared. Mrs. Roth's daughter, Lurline Coonan, was brought up amid these beautiful surroundings, and in her contribution to this book she tells about the new garden she has created at Woodside, California, one steeped in the same tradition, but smaller in scale and consequently more appropriate to a private garden today.

The lesson I learned from Filoli and which I have tried to implement in my own garden in England is the importance of careful tree husbandry and of shaping trees to best advantage. It is good to go away from your own surroundings so that when you return home you see things in a new light. A garden is forever changing and growing and so must constantly be viewed with a critical eye. You

The view across the sunken garden at Filoli toward the coastal range. An avenue of Irish yews wired into columnar shape with a sunburst locust in the distance. Mounds of teucrium mark the corners of the reflecting pool.

can become so accustomed to a tree or shrub that you look at it unquestioningly, when only a few minutes spent shaping it can easily and greatly improve a scene.

Our visit to Elizabeth Lockwood de Forest was memorable. The wife of a famous garden designer, she became an expert on plant associations and color effects and can well be compared with Gertrude Jekyll. Her own garden, sited dramatically with a distant view of an imposing mountain, was full of the best plants that can be grown in Santa Barbara. In 1978 Mrs. de Forest, then in her eighties, replanted the Alice Keck Park Garden, also in Santa Barbara, most imaginatively. She used much ground cover, as is suitable for a public garden. Willowleaf cotoneaster is combined with prostrate rosemary and pyracanthus. The Natal plum and bougainvillea sprawl attractively between the kangaroo vine and the shrimp plant, which in Santa Barbara will flower nonstop through the year. One attractive blue border has plumbago, solanum, statice and tibouchina. With its subtle plant associations, this garden must have considerable influence on those who come to admire or just to walk in it. For myself, I am full of envy for the amazing Santa Barbara climate, which enables plants to grow at twice the speed they do in England, and of course plants that are half-hardy for us grow and flower there for most of the year.

Another important West Coast garden (open to the public by appointment only) is that of Rae Selling Berry in Portland, Oregon. Although we were not able to visit it, I have read about this garden, which epitomizes the collector's garden that is so well represented in this book. Here, sheltered beneath a canopy of 125-year-old Douglas firs, the sixteen-acre garden has a remarkable variety of growing sites and conditions and contains a collection of rare plants. For Mrs. Berry, who possessed a great love and flair for growing things, it was the product of fifty years of planning and planting. Her fine collections of alpines, primulas,

Choice alpines in the rock garden are among the collection of unusual plants in the Rae Selling Berry Botanical Garden in Portland, Oregon.

and rhododendrons, all grown from seed, were augmented through her support of great plant-hunting expeditions earlier in this century, including those of George Forrest and Joseph Rock to China, and of Frank Ludlow and George Sherriff and Sir George Taylor to Tibet. The recent history of this garden is unique, in that Portland is one of the few cities that has succeeded in saving a distinguished garden through the intervention of a group of private citizens with the support of the community. The Friends of the Rae Selling Berry Botanical Garden bought the garden following Mrs. Berry's death in 1977; now not only are plants once threatened with extinction being preserved, but they are being made available to others. The Friends also continue the contributions to the all-important work of present-day plant- and seed-hunting expeditions.

I have promised myself a trip to the Northwest, which has many remarkable gardens, including that of Eulalie Wagner in Tacoma, Washington (see pages 10, 89–93). Mrs. Wagner had the great fortune to grow up in a garden planned by the preeminent designer of the early part of the century, Charles Adams Platt, and then to work herself with one of the most able designers of the mid-century, Thomas Church. As her garden demonstrates, she absorbed their vision and skills but developed her personal style, adapting her conception to her site and making the garden her own.

The Wagner garden may be seen as a link to an earlier tradition, one exemplified by the garden of Mrs. Wagner's parents, the Merrills, in Seattle. The period from 1880 to 1930 was one of intense interest in gardens, when many wealthy Americans created elaborate country estates influenced by travels in Europe and the Orient and by the great international expositions held in the United States. The integrated design approach to house and garden at the turn of the century is splendidly represented in the Merrill garden. It was designed by Charles Platt, probably the greatest interpreter of Italian landscape design in America, and happily the Merrill family is preserving this important example of Italian influence. Mrs. Wagner has written to me about it:

> One of my earliest memories, as a little girl, was waking up the first morning in our new house. The night before we had returned from Europe, having lived there while our house was built. It was a beautiful April morning, and when I peeked into my mother's room, she was leaning out of her west bedroom window overlooking the garden. I still remember her enraptured face. Like most European gardens it is at its best when seen from above. From this vantage point one may take in all the features and dimensions . . . the garden is a visual extension of the house, evoking continuity, order and serenity. From the terrace, formal pathways of white pebbles lead to eight flower beds bordered by dwarf box, forming parterres. On that particular morning, circa 1910, these beds were filled with different colored tulips, all standing at attention, posing as though each flower realized the occasion. Standard bay trees, planted in large wooden boxes, grew at the corners of the parterres, and in the middle of the garden, there was a square grass bed with a

Eulalie Wagner's mother, Eulalee Merrill, brought Charles Platt to Seattle to create an Italianate city garden.

round pool in the center. Some years later this pool was enlivened with an acquisition from Italy, an ancient shell fountain, tended by a cherub blowing water from its horn. There was a formal pergola, vine-covered with wisteria. Eventually this area was embellished with ancestral stone figures obtained from "La Pietra," the celebrated Sir Harold Acton garden near Florence.

Earlier in the century fine gardens were almost always maintained by a number of hired gardeners working to a pattern decided upon by the owners. With the high cost of labor today, many owners do most of the work themselves, and this is often reflected in the diversity and high quality of the planting. Care by owners allows for greater scope and imagination. I am often told that American women want instant and nonupkeep gardens; perhaps it applies to some, but read through this book and you will quickly discover the contrary.

Not only were American women of means commissioning great estate gardens earlier in this century, they were also emerging as talented practitioners of garden design from both apprentice programs and professional schools. In 1915 the

INTRODUCTION

Cambridge School of Architecture and Landscape Architecture for Women was founded in direct response to the fact that women were not permitted to attend classes in these fields at Harvard. Of the work of these first professionals, that of Marion C. Coffin can be seen in this book in the garden of Pamela Copeland in Delaware. Mrs. Coffin was also responsible for much of the design at Winterthur and at two Long Island estates that are now open to the public, Caumsett, the former Marshall Field estate, now owned by the Long Island State Parks Commission, and Clayton, the former Charles Frick estate, now the Nassau Center for the Fine Arts. Annette Hoyt Flanders, who trained at the University of Illinois after her graduation from Smith in 1908, won the 1928 award of the American Society of Landscape Architects for her designs for the McCann estate in Oyster Bay. Some of her private gardens in the Chicago–Milwaukee area where she grew up are still in existence. One of the few women designers of this period who was able to get public commissions was Florence Yock, who created the grounds for the City Hall in Pasadena, California, as well as many private gardens in the area.

Who was the greatest of the American gardening women? Could it have been Beatrix Farrand? Certainly she has left her mark in the American gardening world in much the same way as Gertrude Jekyll has in England. Born in 1872, she traveled widely in Europe. She always wished to be associated with horticulture, and was eventually allowed to work with Charles Sprague Sargent at the Arnold Arboretum. The knowledge of plants she learned from him stood her in good stead when she became a "landscape gardener," as she always called herself. In 1899 she became one of the eleven founding members of the American Society of Landscape Architects. As her reputation grew, her office in New York became ever busier. The two gardens that absorbed her main attention were her own at Reef Point, in Bar Harbor, Maine, and Dumbarton Oaks, in Washington, D.C., where she worked for and with Mrs. Robert Woods Bliss. Reef Point was sold when Mrs. Farrand's husband died, and the garden was destroyed, but Dumbarton Oaks is kept alive in the manner she envisaged.

Beatrix Farrand had a strong and unerring sense of design, which combined with her sensitivity toward plants made her a wonderful gardener. Her plantings were always apparently simple but were characterized by a subtlety that created a harmony and balance that should be analyzed. She liked to use broad-leafed evergreens, such as holly, along with box and yew, to form the structure of her designs. She encouraged the use of indigenous plants and liked subtle softness and unobtrusive symmetry — no surface should be completely flat and no objects completely balanced. Her attention to detail was thorough; she insisted on precise pruning and clipping, but she was strong in her opinion that brick and pavement patterns must be laid not with tape and straight edge, but by eye.

For ten years Mrs. Farrand edited her *Reef Point Garden Bulletin*, which was to guide and instruct gardeners. Its stated object was "to show what outdoor beauty can contribute to those who have the interest and perception that can be influenced by trees and flowers." On every page there are pieces of invaluable advice: "Herbaceous plants must be watched, as there are some that outstay their welcome and spread and lie down on more desirable neighbors." "Good weeding

A rose-covered pergola on the estate of Mrs. Charles E. F. McCann in Oyster Bay, Long Island. Annette Hoyt Flanders received the Gold Medal in Landscape Architecture of the Architectural League of New York for her work here. (Photograph from the glass slide collection of the Garden Club of America)

The original Beatrix Farrand plantings in the Rockefeller garden in Seal Harbor included masses of annuals in the center panel, which is now a closely mown tapis vert *(see page 36).*

Below, a view of Mrs. Farrand's own garden, Reef Point, in Bar Harbor, Maine. (Photographs on this page from the glass slide collection of the Garden Club of America)

consists in taking the offender out literally root and branch." Throughout her garden designs she surely heeded the advice given to her by Charles S. Sargent, "to make the plan fit the ground and not twist the ground to fit the plan."

Beatrix Farrand also made an important contribution of another kind. An admirer of the work of Gertrude Jekyll, she purchased the invaluable collection of Miss Jekyll's notes and papers; they are now in the archives of the University of California in Berkeley.

I have been asked what are some of the fundamental differences between the gardens of American and English women. The answer, of course, lies in our climates, but as the contributors to this book have demonstrated, nothing is too great a challenge. Here in England our weather is much less varied; the west country has a gentler climate than East Anglia, but the differences are nothing compared to the vast range of weather conditions in the United States. It is the elements the gardeners contend with, not their approach, that is different.

Personally I would love to be able to have all manner of half-hardy plants that grow in the warmer zones of the United States, but then I would lose some of the joys that go hand in hand with the reawakening of spring. I would become unhappy with the severe conditions encountered in the cold zones, where the ground is snow-covered or frozen solid for several months each winter, but the American women who live with these conditions have learned to make gardens.

The greatest difference between the two traditions, I believe, is that here in England a far higher percentage of people work in and make gardens than in the United States. Almost every house has a patch that is cultivated, and so garden centers have sprung up in numbers to satisfy the demand for plants. There are just as many "good" gardens in the United States as in England, but there are far fewer carefully cultivated yards around the houses of the town and suburbs. As a result, the demand for plants is less, which leads inevitably to a shortage of garden centers and of available plants. Furthermore, in England gardening seems to be a more general occupation, and in almost every village one or more gardens will be open to the public for charity on some Sunday in the year, under programs organized by the National Gardens Scheme or Red Cross. In addition there are the gardens opened regularly by the owners, when a small admission fee is charged. It has become a national leisure occupation to go "garden visiting," and this in turn generates more interest; people go home and plant another rose, like the one they have just seen. There is no program in the United States comparable to ours, and it has been my experience that in order to see gardens in America you have to be taken by a friend of the owner. Thus, although American gardeners have the same feeling of goodwill and wanting to share as we find here in England, the influence of good gardening is more confined.

In England also we have endless books on gardening, not just practical, how-to books, but books about the ways of creating beautiful effects with your plants, in fact on the aesthetics of the garden. It seems to me that in America there is a scarcity of books concerned with the artistic approach, and even magazine articles are dominated by the how-to aspect.

INTRODUCTION

Beatrix Farrand chose a formal, Italianate approach for the Elipse at Dumbarton Oaks. An aerial hedge of high-pruned American hornbeam trees surrounds an old fountain that Mrs. Bliss found in Provence.

Gertrude Jekyll helped to set a fashion and Vita Sackville-West virtually revolutionized our habits in giving importance to gardening with our own hands, not merely supervising. Most of the contributors to this book do-it-themselves and have expressed their satisfaction in doing so. I love the enthusiasm of the Americans who specialize in herbs, flower decoration, alpines, or vegetables, enthusiasm that comes through clearly in these articles. One is led to feel that if a woman is devoted to her garden there cannot be much wrong with her, be she American or English.

Overleaf: A corner of the garden of Adele Lovett, tightly planted with ground covers (ajuga and alpine strawberries), perennials (mayapple and turtlehead), ferns, and flowering shrubs.

The Gardens

Medora Bass

CASA DEL HERRERO,
SANTA BARBARA, CALIFORNIA

Low walls at the end of the south vista enclose a fountain and plantings of Australian tree ferns and elephant ears, with Raphiolepsis indica *and fuchsias on the lower level.*

CASA DEL HERRERO means the House of the Blacksmith. Our place got its name because manufacturing metal products was my father's business and he jokingly referred to himself as a blacksmith. I often think how fortunate I was to inherit a Spanish house and garden in one of the loveliest spots in all the world.

My first memories of the garden are of seeing a blueprint of a semicircle of hedges enclosing a long lawn leading to a fountain. Outside the hedges were squiggles for trees — orange trees, I was told. The site was an old Spanish land grant, halfway between the mountains and the sea, and my mother was concerned because the garden would slope downhill instead of uphill as a proper garden should.

The house and garden were begun in 1922, and my perfectionist father wanted both to be authentically Spanish. I remember hearing the names of Ralph Stevens, Peter Riedel, and Lockwood de Forest in connection with the garden, and over and over again, the name of the architect, George Washington Smith. My father worked constantly on the blueprints. He made a trip to Spain, accompanied by Arthur Byne and his wife Mildred Stapley, authorities on Spanish gardens and antiques, and in five weeks was able to buy tiles, grilles, Moorish doors, furniture, tapestries, stone carvings, and even a fifteenth-century ceiling from a monastery. For the garden there were enormous flowerpots and wrought-iron gates. He took photographs and made sketches in Seville, Granada, Ronda, and Majorca. Then it was back to the blueprints to incorporate all these into the plans.

The garden went through many changes; the sound of the tile setters' hammers was almost constant even after we moved in during the summer of the 1925 earthquake. If a pergola was to be added or a tree moved, a mock-up was built to ensure that the perspective and the proportions satisfied my mother and father. The project was my father's dream, but he always respected my mother's advice.

The next twenty years were spent developing the house and garden. My father had so many ideas that he had apprentices working full time with him in a well-equipped shop. Among the products were aluminum garden furniture in the Spanish style and lion finials for the terrace railings. Later silversmithing became

Jasmine overhanging the benches and massed oleanders perfume a tiled exedra. Heliotrope and blue felicia bloom in the blue and white border. To the north is the Santa Ynez coastal range.

A pavement at the Alhambra inspired the pebble pattern of the entry court. The rare Bolivian vine Distictis laxifolia *drapes the eaves of the house. The shorter palms are* Chamaerops humilis, *and the taller, with philodendron climbing the trunks, are* Phoenix roebelinii. *Pots of ivy-leaved geraniums surround the pool.*

his absorbing hobby after the garden was completed. His finest pieces were sculptured vases to display mother's camellias, beautifully inscribed "To hold God's gifts for your delight."

My mother was devastated by my father's death and I believe it was gardening that restored her to her cheerful, gracious self. She became quite a horticulturist, was president of the Santa Barbara Garden Club and won prizes in the flower shows. Every morning she would inspect the gardens with our loyal gardener and horticulturist, Joe Acquistapace, and then worked in the rose garden. Roses and camellias were her favorite arrangements. One of my father's last projects was to set up a darkroom so the flower arrangements could be photographed before they went to the house; he hated to have such beauty be so fleeting.

When my mother died in 1963, my husband's business kept us in the East for a time, and it would not have been possible for me to keep up the place without the dedicated help of the two head gardeners. Joe worked here for almost fifty years, and he trained Ildo Marra, the son of one of the old gardeners, who returned after graduation from college. I always feel that the garden has only been loaned to me and that it really belongs to those who created and nurtured it. I

California oaks (Quercus agrifolia) frame the view of the house from the lower end of the south vista. Two Raphiolepsis indica *flank the steps. The vine on the house is copa de oro* (Solandra rigata).

have the joy of getting most of my exercise in it now that I have given up tennis and I have inherited my mother's tasks in the rose garden.

A visit to the garden begins in the spacious white-walled front courtyard with a Spanish tiled pool and a black-and-white pebbled pavement similar to that of the Patio de la Reja in the Alhambra. On either side of the entrance gate are medium-sized gray palms, *Butia capitata*; on the west wall is a mass of treelike bird-of-paradise plants (*Strelitzia nicolai*), and along the south side of the court are tall kentia palms with dracaenas against the house. The foundation planting also includes the short bushy palm, *Chamaerops humilis,* a delicate Roebelin palm (*Phoenix roebelinii*), and an enormous philodendron that climbs the palms.

A wrought-iron gate set in the east side of the court leads you to the camellia garden with statues of a saint and a satyr at either end. From here, steps lead through an arch in the pittosporum hedge into our only formal flower garden. At one end is a large exedra with colorful tiled benches under the overhanging pittosporum; at the other is a pergola covered with a banksia rose. On either side of the narrow lawn are borders of perennials, mostly blue and white. Almost solid rows of agapanthus are interspersed with calla lilies, iris, statice, heliotrope, Jap-

Sheared eugenia hedges underplanted with ivy and scallops of star jasmine border the south lawn.

anese anemones, and shasta daisies. I try to keep a low edging of pansies, petunias, primroses, lobelia, candytuft, and dianthus. The many white flowers are in memory of my parents, who often enjoyed the garden in the moonlight.

Halfway down the east side of this garden is another colorful sitting area with tiled benches on either side of a tall decorative panel. White oleanders arch above the benches and jasmine scrambles over the backs. Curved stairs descend to a fan-shaped rose garden filled only with tree roses, which give it the medieval look my father loved.

From the rose garden, the path leads up again to the rose-covered pergola and on through the arches of the walled garden. In this small "sitting garden" with brick and tile paving there is a central fountain and geometric beds now planted with small-leaved English ivy for easier maintenance. The walls are completely covered with creeping fig and topped by a Cecile Brunner rose. A bench with a view of the ocean and the islands through the south archway is one of my favorite spots in the late afternoon. I have reached an age now when all I collect are sunsets.

The central green vista slopes south from the house, ornamented by a tiled star pool and a gothic birdhouse cum sundial with the motto: "Use well thy time/ fast fly the hours/ Good works live on." Eugenia hedges, bordered with bands of ivy and scallops of star jasmine, extend to the fern garden and its fountain. Down a few steps is a smaller walled garden of tree ferns, camellias, and fuchsias. I am experimentally replacing the grass in the small center plot with Korean moss, which requires less water and almost no mowing. A gate beyond leads to the cactus garden, which is dominated by tall clumps of dragon trees (*Dracaena draco*) which seem to date from the time of the dinosaurs.

From the lower end of the garden we usually walk back on the west side outside the formal hedges, through citrus and other fruit trees along a path bordered by agapanthus. The trees flourish thanks to a Depression-era project. Jobless men drifted in every day then asking for work, and since my father already employed eight gardeners, new work had to be found to help out. The drainage of the clay soil was poor and orange trees hate wet feet, so the job-seekers were put to work digging trenches and laying pipes to drain each tree. They also built compost bins and garbage pits, as organic gardening was practiced here many years before it became popular elsewhere.

This year, at seventy-three, I have become acutely aware of the passing of time and the changes it imposes on me and the garden. The box hedges my mother loved in the rose garden outlived her by twenty years, but had to be removed recently. Our stately yews also died of some unidentified fungus and I mourn their passing. I am undecided whether to replace the box with other low hedges, perhaps of euonymus or rosemary. Shall I replace the yew with cypress? That would preserve one of the characteristics of the Spanish gardens — the enclosure of each area so that the next part is a surprise. Joe, who still acts as a consultant at eighty plus, keeps reminding me of this, but I seem to prefer more open views. It was comforting to read in *The Englishwoman's Garden* that several women who inherited gardens had difficulty developing the confidence to impose their own ideas

Creeping fig (Ficus repens) *upholsters the arches of the walled garden. Petunias and agapanthus flower in the blue and white border, which is across the grass from the one shown on page 22. The south lawn is through the arches.*

and wishes onto the designs of their forebears. It took me five years to cut down the specimen live oaks in front of the patio. They darkened the house and blocked our view of the ocean. Now I can lie in bed and see the sunrise on the ocean. But will the less stately orange trees I have planted look as well?

I wonder if I am realistic in hoping that someone in the family will be able to afford to keep up Casa del Herrero. And I worry that I am neglecting my reading and work in the population and family planning field. But then I remember the old Chinese proverb that ends "if you want to be happy for life, plant a garden."

Blue vitex, 'Hyperion' daylilies, and white yarrow in the perennial border.

May in the flower yard, with Rosa mutabilis *blooming on the fence and pansies within the patterned box. The shrub in the corner is the tea plant* (Camellia sinensis) *once imported to Georgia as an economic plant. Virginia creeper clothes the chimney.*

Jane Symmes

CEDAR LANE FARM, MADISON, GEORGIA

EACH YEAR that I garden at Cedar Lane Farm, I appreciate more and more how fortunate I am to be doing what I enjoy most at this particular place in the world. Here in the Georgia piedmont we have tremendous advantages of a varied climate and a long growing season, provided we are sure of an adequate water supply and the ability to apply it. Sometimes, when the thermometer hits 100°, I wonder if I will have the energy to drag another hose.

Cedar Lane came into existence because John, my late husband, wished to grow distinctive trees and shrubs for the nursery industry, and I had always wanted to restore an old house. So, to fulfill these dreams, we bought a farm in Madison, Georgia, in 1966. The acreage included an old spring smothered in honeysuckle, and an 1830s "plantation plain" house, stacked to the ceiling with bales of hay.

Before we really began on the house and gardens, John designed the layout for the nursery. Top priority went to making a lake by damming the spring. We were most interested in growing plants indigenous to the southeastern United States. There are so many excellent ones neglected by the nursery trade that we felt a mission to encourage their use. We also sought to select the sources of our cuttings to assure cold hardiness as well as superior forms and colors. Among the non-natives, we found a very cold-hardy Confederate jasmine (*Trachelospermum jasminoides*) and an unusually deep blue vitex (*V. agnus-castus*), a shrub sometimes known as summer lilac.

While John was organizing the nursery, I began researching, as I wanted to respect the historic integrity of the house in its restoration. The plantation-plain style is a vernacular simplification of the eighteenth-century Virginia tidewater house transplanted to the farmlands of the piedmont. Typically this is a modest two-story four-room house formally divided by a center hall often leading (as does ours) to a single-story rear section. Clapboard walls, exterior end chimneys, and a gabled roof identify the style.

I also wanted to reclaim the grounds around the house in the manner of a nineteenth-century Georgia plantation, using a characteristic layout and growing plants of the period. I remember a friend who is a landscape architect telling me that such a scheme was only a silly academic exercise. Perhaps it was, but it led to some fascinating reading and many delightful field trips to old gardens.

Beebalm and horseradish in a corner of the kitchen garden in late June. The perennial border beyond is filled with heat-resistant plants: from left to right, the pink-flowering old shrub Chinquapin Rose (R. Roxburghii), the classic 'Hyperion' daylily, deep golden rudbeckia, tall spires of white sweet rocket (Hesperis matronalis), and blue salvia.

I began my researches with the remarkable *Garden History of Georgia*, published in 1933 by the Peachtree Garden Club. I kept reading old volumes like Robert Squibbs's *Gardener's Calendar*, Bernard McMahon's *American Gardener*, and Robert Buist's *American Flower Garden Directory*. I then began to realize the value of periodicals, diaries, and letters for information about the actual plantings. The manuscript diary of a friend's great-great-grandmother described dahlias and vitex in DeBruce, Georgia, in 1848. An 1838 letter from Texas described growing Carolina jessamine up a redbud tree.

Finding varieties that look like illustrations in nineteenth-century books has meant searching out old houses and garden sites. Tenant houses on out-of-the-way plantations have been the sources of many old-fashioned flowers, and abandoned cemeteries have yielded old box and rose varieties. My friend Florence Griffin, who created the enchanting gardens of the Tullie Smith House on the grounds of the Atlanta Historical Society, is a great plant detective and brings me many of her special finds as tiny cuttings in plastic bags. Fortunately I can use the mist house in the nursery to propagate these cuttings. A special treasure is the cutleaf Persian lilac (*Syringa laciniata*), the one lilac that is happy in the South.

HISTORIC GARDENS

Interest in old plants has led me to develop a special catalogue of native and introduced plants for historic gardens. The enthusiastic response to this list indicates that the idea of restoring grounds as well as buildings is coming of age. The recent organization of a Southern Garden History Society modeled on the English society will surely encourage more garden restoration.

When John and I finally began to work on the grounds around the house, the topography had us puzzled, and erosion had eradicated most evidence of original gardens. The old drive came quite close to the north-facing front door, and the sloping terrain in front of the house seemed to preclude the possibility that the typical fenced flower yard was ever there. So we placed the picket-fenced flower garden on the west or parlor side of the house, and on the east or service side we put a small kitchen garden, also with palings. Some fifty feet from the rear of the house we set out a long perennial border backed with chestnut rails set in zigzag fashion. Beyond is a large vegetable garden and a small orchard. Although we did not reproduce the complete nineteenth-century layout, the various fences and out buildings suggest the plantation atmosphere.

In the flower yard, however, I was determined to try for a true nineteenth-century effect by edging the simply patterned beds with English box that I rooted from bushes in John's grandmother's garden. Here I grow pansies, which I adore. The rabbits do too. When asked if I plant them in the fall or spring, I reply, "Both. In the fall for the rabbits and in the spring for me." Here are old favorites like foxgloves, *Kerria japonica*, and *Rosa mutabilis*, which changes from tight apricot buds to bright pink petals that deepen to near magenta when full blown. The chinensis ancestry of this old species rose gives it repeated flushes of bloom and the coppery red of the young leaves and stems add to the harlequin effect. Natives are also featured here: columbine (*Aquilegia canadensis*), *Phlox divaricata*, piedmont azaleas (*Rhododendron canescens*), blue-leaved St. John's wort (*Hypericum frondosum*), and the lovely blue-flowering *Amsonia tabernaemontana*. Enjoying these blooms and the charming yellow woodbine honeysuckle (*Lonicera sempervirens* 'Sulphurea') on the picket fence, I am always pleased to think how much of the exquisite beauty of spring is native to this country.

This garden needed a windbreak because of miles of open farm land to the west, and we chose the beautiful American holly selection, *Ilex opaca* 'Carolina #2'. I know Christopher Lloyd says never plant holly as a hedge behind beds that must be weeded, but the deep green foliage and generous berry crop make this variety worth pricked fingers. This is the garden I love; I like to smell the boxwood and see its pattern blanketed with snow; I like to recall Easter egg hunts here when my daughters were small. And I like to weed. Weeding here has a special satisfaction because at least in a confined space one can bring order and harmony, evicting the unwanted and unpleasant so that the wanted and pleasant can flourish. Such an accomplishment is rare beyond the garden fence. I certainly subscribe to the idea that the patterned garden was so popular in nineteenth-century Georgia because it was like an oasis in pushing back the wilderness.

The long border is richer in texture, color, and variety since Treadwell Rice Crown III came on board in 1982 to assist me in managing the nursery. An

Variegated English holly and an old white German iris on either side of the chestnut rail fence of the perennial border. Beyond the vegetable garden is the lake with the pumphouse for the nursery. The tall shrub is Euonymus alatus.

outstanding plantsman who grew up knowing his grandmother's distinguished garden, Rick has shared his scholarly knowledge and infectious enthusiasm in both nursery and garden and has added many wonderful plants from his own collection. We are learning that if we can make the proper choices for our climate, which is Zone 8a according to the U.S. Department of Agriculture, and "changeable" according to gardeners, we can have a wealth of material over a long blooming season. At Cedar Lane, Canadian hemlock and Bartram's Florida anise tree both flourish, as do figs, pomegranates, and raspberries.

Operating the nursery full time, as I have since John died in 1973, leaves little time for gardening. There are still areas I would like to develop, but realistically I have to limit myself, for maintenance is time-consuming and help is scarce. There can be no natural woodland gardens in the South without constantly battling the invasive Japanese honeysuckle. The quantities I alone have pulled up would make a sizable mountain, and my epitaph might read, "She died fighting *Lonicera japonica*." I lie awake nights dreaming of a hillside garden above the spring planted with the native azaleas we are propagating in the nursery. There would also be silver-bell trees (*Halesia carolina*), sweetspire shrubs (*Itea virginica*), oconee bells (*Shortia galacifolia*), and other southern delights. One day my daughters may work toward this goal, as they seem to share their parents' enthusiasm for gardens. But until an irrigation system is in place we can only dream.

The old spring that bubbles up from large exposed rocks is truly the heart of Cedar Lane. The Indians knew it, as evidenced by quantities of arrowheads nearby; the original builder of the house was drawn by the spring's proximity and we purchased the farm because it would provide irrigation for the nursery. The hot, hot days of summer only intensify the feeling in my heart that knows that without this life-giving source there would be neither the nursery nor the gardens I love.

A brief winter snowfall outlines the nineteenth-century geometry of the flower yard.

THE GARDEN OF

Peggy Rockefeller

THE ABBY ALDRICH ROCKEFELLER GARDEN
SEAL HARBOR, MAINE

I N 1921 my parents-in-law, Abby Aldrich Rockefeller and John D. Rockefeller, Jr., took a three-month trip to China, Japan, and Korea, where they came under the spell of oriental art. This was to be an abiding influence on each of them — and a great source of pleasure, I am sure — for the rest of their lives. Certainly the oriental influence in the Abby Aldrich Rockefeller Garden is directly attributable to that trip. The garden was started in 1924 or 1925, and Mrs. Rockefeller worked very closely with Beatrix Farrand, our most celebrated woman landscape gardener. Mrs. Rockefeller was neither a botanist nor a horticulturist, but she had a wonderful eye for color and design. Mrs. Farrand was extraordinarily erudite and botanically knowledgeable, and the two ladies made a marvelous team.

The garden was carved out of a spruce-covered hilltop in Seal Harbor, Maine. An area close to two acres was cleared and leveled, and of course the soil had to be brought "from away," a huge task. The original plan was for an "English Garden." But while this was in the making, the Rockefellers had not dropped their interest in oriental art forms, and they had begun to collect Chinese sculpture, Korean stone figures, and Japanese stone lanterns. Most of these were procured through Yamanaka and Company, which had started a branch in Bar Harbor, Maine. I can see why! Plans for extensions of the garden included new areas that were to be oriental in feeling, and my parents-in-law bought a large number of burnt-orange or "imperial yellow" tiles that came from the Forbidden City of Peking, where sections of its walls were being torn down. Today these tiles surmount the rosy-pink stucco wall that surrounds the garden on three sides, looking just like their counterparts that one can still see in Peking.

One enters the garden through heavy wooden doors in this wall and looks down, or walks along, a gravel path between a double row of Korean tomb figures surrounded by ground covers of mosses, mountain cranberry, blueberries, and bunchberries. The path leads to a fifth-century Chinese stele set in a small opening where one gets a view, or really just a glimpse, of a lake far below. Or one could turn left immediately, to walk along a tiny path through ferns and mossy rocks to a Chinese shrine. On turning right from the main entrance, one follows a path of stones laid in moss and leading through a bottle gate in a wall that partially divides

Korean tomb figures preside over a carpet of native Maine mosses, mountain cranberries, blueberries, and bunchberries along the Spirit Walk.

The soft mauves of the tall thalictrum
'Hewitt's Double' and mats of ageratum
'Blue Blazer' and heliotrope 'Royal
Fragrance' in subtle harmony with walls
inspired by those of the Forbidden City
in Peking. 'White Admiral' phlox and
dianthus 'Snowfire' highlight the
plantings.

A panoramic view north from the oval garden, with the pastel borders on the west and the vivid ones on the east.

the formal planted garden from the first area, which is essentially wild. Stepping through the bottle gate one is in an all-green oval garden where it seems natural to lower one's voice to a whisper. It is an oasis of green lawn surrounded by low green plants and shrubs (no-color borders) with a background of birches, maples, laburnum, moosewood, and spruce. A small reflecting pool is at one end of the oval and there is a strange feeling of peace and quiet here. If one crosses this area, another little path leads into a quiet sanctuary where one can sit and contemplate a very lovely eleventh-century Chinese marble figure.

Look north from the oval and there you will see the original flower garden, a large sunken rectangular lawn, and English borders. This lawn is edged on all four sides by beds of annuals, backed by low stone walls. There are more beds of annuals along the wall tops and then across a path on this higher level an herbaceous border and *another* stone wall. Have I lost you? The east and west sides of the garden are designed in somewhat similar fashion, melting finally into a spruce woods. But at the north end there appears again the tiled wall, with a moon gate in the middle. A huge spruce tree stands sentinel before it, and the area is planted once more in non-colors; mauve, white, gray, green, to reflect the quiet feeling of the oval at the south end.

The non-color area serves another purpose as well. The garden was always planted, and still is, with all the hot colors (reds, oranges, yellows, purples, etc.) on the east side, and all the pastel shades of pink, blue, lilac, white, and so forth on the west side. The moon gate area separates these two and gives one a chance to readjust before crossing over to the opposite spectrum. Another transition is made by strong groups of dark blue delphiniums in the corners. Their spires take the eye up to the next level. And clematis trained on the walls helps link flowers of the same colors in the upper and lower levels.

A bright mix of zinnias and red annual phlox, blue delphinium and salvia, and yellow rudbeckia on the "hot" side of the garden.

The two levels of the cool border, where varieties of phlox, verbena, pansies, violas, ageratums, petunias, alyssums, snapdragons, campanulas, penstemon, anchusa, and delphinium are among the flowers that create a color scheme of blues, grays, lilacs, pink, and pale yellow. The plantings in the upper left are now predominantly perennial.

Mrs. Rockefeller worked very closely with Mrs. Farrand on the plans for this garden and the subsequent planting of it. As with all gardens, it changed from time to time and undoubtedly would have continued to do so had she lived. She died in 1948, and the garden had little family supervision until 1960, when my husband, David, asked me to take it over. I had always loved gardening, but knowledge and love do not necessarily go hand in hand and there has been much to learn. There were complicating factors as well. This garden had always been planned and planted to be in full bloom from July 15 to September 5, when the family would have their summer holiday in Seal Harbor, and the time when all right-minded "summer folk" would be there. Nowadays, summer folk come any old time and stay longer, but the garden is still right-minded and is strictly a seven-week affair. What problems that produces! We can't grow any of the early-blooming perennials, and anything that is so rash as to bloom after Labor Day is soon pulled out by the roots. No use planting lovely spring bulbs or wonderful late aconites. Oh, dear!

Originally, the garden was 85 percent annuals, and that made life easier. But three years ago my husband and I visited a wonderful group of English gardens

Neutral shades provide a transition between the contrasting color schemes on each side of the garden, with lobelia 'Crystal Palace' left of the spruce trunk and 'Cambridge Blue' to the right of it, amid ajuga and viola 'Blue Perfection'. Verbena amethyst on the right path leading to the moongate and a mass of Hosta lancifolia in bloom on the path to the left add more mauves, while ageratum 'Summer Snow', petunias, annual white phlox, and the silver foliage of nepeta, stachys, and dusty miller provide cooling accents.

with Rosemary Verey and Sybil Connolly and were totally seduced by the beauty and variety of their herbaceous borders. Nothing would do but that we should try the same thing in Seal Harbor, only their blooming time had to be condensed. The first year was trial and error. Out of three kinds of plants, one would bloom in June, another in *late* September and the third would give up the ghost at the very thought of a Maine winter. But perseverance and a marked increase in humility have paid off, and at last the two perennial borders are beginning to look, well, *better*.

The garden is now open to the public on Wednesdays (from July 15 to September 5, of course), and we anticipate endowing it so that it may continue to give pleasure and perhaps even instruction to those who venture within.

People ask how we plan the garden from year to year; do we change it? Indeed we do. As the summer draws to a close, our head gardener, Gary Solari, and I get out an easel and the big boards on which he has sketched in the summer's plan of every part of the garden. Out comes the gingerbread and coffee, we stand facing the plan looking at the real thing behind it, and then we go over all of it with a fine-tooth comb. Color comes first. Should we leave it as it is or change

Looking from the Spirit Walk to the entry gate roofed with "imperial yellow" tiles from Peking.

it? Then we check for height, for texture, for accents, and for season of bloom. Having planned everything to the last inch and ordered the seeds, then come the changes, the tearing of hair as old standbys suddenly become unobtainable, the despair as our favorite seed house goes out of business, etc. In fact, it is no different from any other garden, and I wouldn't have it any other way. Well, maybe a *little* different. . . .

Alice Callaway

HILLS AND DALES, LA GRANGE, GEORGIA

M Y GREAT LOVE of gardening started fifty years ago, when my husband and I built our first house. The architect, Ernest Ivey, designed a charming small rose and perennial garden enclosed by a picket fence, with a pool in the center of a grass plot. Three years later, after the death of both my husband's parents, we moved to their home, Hills and Dales. The change to caring for five and a half acres instead of a quarter acre, at age twenty-three, was an awesome one. Through the years I have learned by experience and by keeping records, as well as by reading many gardening books. I work outside every day when the weather permits, and in the winter the greenhouse gives me many happy and fruitful hours of potting, rooting, and training plants.

Our Boxwood Garden is 142 years old and has seen many changes as well as many helpers. If the magnolia, ginkgo, and cunninghamnia trees could talk, what stories they could tell! Sara Coleman Ferrell, who laid out the original plan, started this garden when she was in her twenties; she lived to be eighty-seven, and worked all those years to establish and maintain its unusual design. Ten years after Mrs. Ferrell's death my father-in-law, Fuller Callaway, bought the property, which by then had become so overgrown that it required careful clearing even to locate the original paths. Today, the paths and beds are just as Mrs. Ferrell developed them, but with changes in plant material relating to the architecture of the present house, built in 1916.

Fuller Callaway knew Mrs. Ferrell and came often to visit her in her garden. When he bought the property, he removed the Victorian one-story house, replacing it with an Italian villa in keeping with the terraces and formal garden, and named it Hills and Dales because of the rolling land surrounding the house. He had only twelve years to enjoy and act upon his vision of making an even more beautiful garden before he died, in 1928. His widow, Ida Cason Callaway, cared for and loved the garden until her death in 1936. It then became my responsibility to love and care for this treasure. Fortunately, for a novice, I also inherited some dedicated old-time helpers who carried me through the early years of my ignorance. Since my grandmother and my mother were ardent gardeners, I had grown up with a love for gardening, so to me it was never work, and to see the results of my labor gave me great pleasure.

The bunch of grapes in the oldest part of the garden at the west end of the fifth level was a Victorian symbol of the fruitful land of Canaan.

The five terraces ascending to the Italianate villa are seen from the sunken garden on the sixth level. The massed crimson azaleas on second level are Kurume 'Hino Giri.'

The formal Boxwood Garden comprises six terraces running east to west, with the steps and retaining walls made of native stone. A beautiful semicircular dry stone wall curves around the sunken garden on the sixth terrace. The view from a stone bench here, looking up the terraces to the house and upper fountain, is one of the most admired in the whole garden.

Mrs. Ferrell was fond of boxwood mottoes, a feature of garden design that goes back to Roman gardens described by Pliny. She was obviously a very religious person, and the word "God" spelled out in box at the entry of the garden was her tribute to the glory of God that she found within. Just as the first verses of Genesis begin with his name, so did her garden. To show that it was also her promised land, she planted an enormous bunch of grapes symbolizing the fruit that the Israelite scouts brought out of the land of Canaan. (Family Bibles of the time often were illustrated with engravings of Joshua and Caleb carrying oversized bunches of grapes.) Each grape is a small box bush. The earliest part of the garden was the "Church Garden," which Mrs. Ferrell furnished with a pipe organ, harp, pulpit, two mourners' benches, and a collection plate, all in box. I plant this garden entirely in white, from the azaleas and wisterias of spring, through the hostas and oleanders of late summer.

Immediately in front of the house, Sara Ferrell planted separate boxwood emblems for herself and her husband. The words "God is Love" formed hers, and the Masonic symbol and the words "Fiat Justitia" were for Judge Ferrell, who was a Mason. It is said that Mrs. Ferrell saved the place from destruction by Union soldiers after the last battle of the War between the States (fought at West Point, Georgia, eighteen miles to the south), by personally leading their commander, who was also a Mason, to see this planting.

One change that I made was to plant the garden adjacent to the greenhouse

Concentric circles of box and the Kurume azalea 'Snow' ring the fountain on the upper terrace.

with herbs; the area, in full sun, is perfect for them. A well-known herb specialist, Rosemary Louden, redesigned the planting of this garden last year, and a program for reworking the beds was begun. The garden shows great improvement in health and beauty from the addition of peat moss, sawdust, and lime to the soil before the plants were reset. Despite our hot, dry Georgia summers, little watering is needed, and the only maintenance necessary is cutting off dead blooms and trimming the plants occasionally. The garden is conveniently located near the kitchen door, so it is ideal for gathering culinary herbs.

Another addition has been a garden below the entry drive, in full view of the courtyard and seen by everyone coming to the house. The beds are in a spoke design, with a lacy metal gazebo covered with clematis in the center. It is easily maintained, with grass paths between the beds filled with plants chosen for both flower and foliage: azaleas, iris, *Alyssum saxatile,* variegated liriope, and daylilies. Hemlock hedges and seventy-year-old pecan trees beyond frame the scene.

Our most colorful time is in April, when the Kurume and Indica azaleas are in bloom. The new green growth on the boxwood adds to the freshness of the

The motto "God" was the earliest planting at the original entrance to the garden at the east end of the fifth terrace. Alice Callaway added the statue of Saint Fiacre, patron saint of gardens, to the old patterns.

season, and the long vistas are especially effective, with the old stone statuary and benches lending an aura of age and a touch of classic beauty. The white dogwood and white wisteria are a lovely contrast to the blue sky. A few late blooms of blue and white scilla and white violets are dotted about. Dove trees bloom in the sunken garden, a rare sight in any Georgia garden. The yellow Lady Banksia rose festoons the trunk of a straight old ash tree. Perfume from the blossoms of the banana shrub (*Michelia fuscata*) fills the air and invokes childhood memories of tying their petals in a handkerchief to put under my pillow to induce sweet dreams.

We try to plan for the stress caused by long dry summers and falls, but it is the damage to young foliage and flowers caused by sudden cold snaps after a warm spell in winter or early spring that is most discouraging. Our normal minimum winter temperature is 10° to 20°, but such cold does not linger and we often have camellias blooming with snow on the ground in January and February. The rare occasions when the temperature drops to 10° below zero cause severe damage and after the cold of 1982 many of our camellias, fifty years old or more, had to be drastically pruned. We hope that with loving care they will return to their former beauty. One of the greatest hazards in a garden with huge old magnolia trees is that when any rare snow or ice appears, the limbs, very heavy and brittle, may crack and fall on the boxwood, causing great damage to borders and hedges. Boxwood requires a minimum of care for such a hardy and long-lived evergreen. It is pruned once a year, and afterwards is given a feeding of cottonseed meal. If the summer is dry, watering must be done in July and August. Some plants are lost each year despite the best of care, but for the number grown, the loss is infinitesimal.

Since the great hundred-year-old *Magnolia grandiflora* cast so much shade and their roots go out in all directions, it is difficult to have blooming plants in the beds in the summer. They are filled then with ground covers: vinca minor, ajuga, mondo grass, variegated liriope, and pachysandra, to name a few. They make a nice contrast to the boxwood. Stone urns placed strategically are filled with geraniums and other blooming pot plants for color in the summer. Tender potted oleanders and bougainvillea are moved out in warm weather to decorate other spots. The paths are covered with gravel.

The main joy of gardening for me, aside from growing beautiful, healthy plants, is finding rare ones and growing them successfully. Such a plant is the *Magnolia delavayi* growing on the south side of the house. It has beautiful foliage and blooms over the longest period of any magnolia I know. Now I have four two-year rooted plants to set out elsewhere. Whenever we take a trip, I visit gardens and nurseries, and usually come home with a few plants to add to our collection. A cryptomeria was brought home in the back seat of the car many, many years ago, and is now fifty feet tall.

If I had known what my future would be while I was in college, I certainly would have studied botany and horticulture. Books provide a wealth of information, however, and I believe that experience is the greatest teacher.

Golden yarrow fills one of the beds in the herb garden alongside the greenhouse and workrooms.

Salvia, coreopsis, and pansies in the June border.

A curved entry walk invites visitors in from the street for the April show of azaleas and tulips. Statuary and clipped box offer year-round interest.

THE GARDEN OF

Emily Whaley

CHARLESTON, SOUTH CAROLINA

T HE OLD SAYING "It's an ill wind that blows nobody good" applies to me. You will see why.

Our Charleston town garden is thirty by fifty feet and is behind the house, almost invisible from the street. Many years ago we employed Loutrell Briggs, the landscape architect, to draw a plan, asking him to arrange the garden in self-contained areas so that I could go ahead with one section at a time. I was pleased with his design. He had laid out the area in circles of different sizes that completely obscured the fact that it was a tiny, narrow terrain.

I started with the section at the back of the lot, which was blessed with two assets: a prettily shaped oak tree that made an arched canopy over the back garden and a brick carriage house on the rear boundary, which gave us privacy. The plan called for raised borders around a circle of brick, creating the effect of a sunken garden. The shade and the raised borders were made to order for camellias and azaleas. I had first loves among the camellias and planted three pairs. When choosing the azaleas, I went wild. Each time I saw an unfamiliar variety, I thought it the most beautiful I'd ever seen and I bought reds, salmons, pinks, lavenders — you name it, they were there in my circle. They made a glorious display and for many years that part of the garden was highly satisfactory to me.

The next section, put in several years later, contained a circular pool one and a half inches deep. This seemed to be a magnet for the birds and often there would be fifteen splashing in it. In the area in front of this I planted two candy-striped peach trees and two variegated pittosporum. Along one side green pittosporum were interspersed with George Taber azaleas; on the opposite border camellias were interspersed with a few azaleas. In spring, each border was lined with Aristocrat tulips, Wedgwood blue iris, stock, snapdragons, and blue salvia, all of which bloom at varying times until the end of May.

The traditional cut-off date for gardening in Charleston is June first, when the superheated humidity of summer envelops us and many of us steal away to our barrier islands for the next three months, leaving our gardens to become the land of sleeping beauty. The vines, the volunteers, and the voluminous growth take over. When I get back to the garden in September, I am always astonished. Each year I think *this* time I am not going to be able to get it back to shape; there

is no possible way to do it. But with a good man on a ladder, a helper on the ground, and me moving around to view each cut from every angle, we are back to normal in a day or two. The process always amazes me.

After many years I put in a patio. I didn't plan this carefully enough and did an unimaginative job. I was bogged down with family matters, debuts and weddings, and in truth I had become more or less bored with gardening. This situation lasted for five years or so and then suddenly the whole thing changed. We had a storm with heavy winds. Large limbs were ripped from the sugarberry tree in the back of the garden, and fell on the camellias and azaleas. Everything in that area was left a shambles. A tree expert patched up the sugarberry tree and we pruned the injured camellias and azaleas, but after a year we could see that they would never recover their beauty. At this point, another vicious storm struck. It finished off the sugarberry, which fell on the candy-striped peach trees.

Now I had to make a decision. Did I have the desire or time to redo the garden properly? Did we have enough unallocated money to replant it properly? My husband decided that the garden should be replanted, and he promised not to have a nervous breakdown over what I spent.

A view of the yard from the patio in April. Lavender azaleas flower in the circular back garden. Unseen beyond is "Mrs. Whaley's Lovers' Lane" of ferns, swamp iris, and wildflowers.

CITY AND TOWN

The decision turned me once again into an avid gardener. I employed excellent help and in no time the garden was cleared of all injured plants. What a relief! Now I could assess the possibilities and correct former mistakes. We still had the live oak, the original ground plan, the mellow brick, and some large surviving plants for backgrounds to new plantings.

My goal was twofold: first, to plant the garden from front to back in seven sections — the three sections designed by Loutrell Briggs and four additional sections that would challenge my imagination, my design ability, and my horticultural know-how. I felt these four new individual gardens would add variety, add focal points as well as giving me a great deal of pleasure. Second, since the Spoleto Festival now brings visitors in June, I wanted plant material that would extend the blooming period.

Again I started in the back circle, planting a few camellias interspersed with blue hydrangeas. We took out a mass of salmon azaleas and replaced them with the George Tabers. We also added azaleas in two shades of pink and a number of whites. In the spring I tuck in white impatiens. This area now remains lovely from January through July.

In the next two sections we planted parkinsonias, which bloom from May to July. At each end of the two twenty-foot borders are urns full of blooming plants and by each urn a yellow floribunda rose is planted.

The patio with pots of impatiens, geraniums, and Bavarian bells is pretty, comfortable, and inviting. Walking out toward the entrance gate we come on a new area. A shallow pool with two cranes wading in it and a turtle watching carefully is surrounded by four varieties of fern, some wood violets, ginger, and ajuga. The background of fatsia, myrtle, and *Mahonia fortunei* gives a slightly tropical appearance. Next is a small contained area where a statue of a girl with a shell full of water at her feet is backed by a boxwood and surrounded by bleeding heart plants. The seventh area, which one of my helpers calls "Mrs. Whaley's Lover's Lane," is tucked in at the very back and filled with ferns.

Now you see that ill wind blew me a great deal of good. Today, at age seventy-two, I am really just beginning to get my sea legs in my own garden, but I find it lots of fun. It's a project you can't leave alone — you're digging and planting and your hair is a sight, your fingers are grimy, and blessedly you don't even realize you're exercising. And then there is the wonderful conversation with your gardening friends, the exchange of ideas, and the discussions of your and their never-ending experiments, excitements, discoveries, and pleasures. It beats gossip any hour of the day. It beats gossip any day of the week.

And one last admonition: Don't let anyone, man, woman, or child, organize your time for you. If you do, you'll be sure to find yourself up to your elbows in dishwater or sitting on two or three committees or simply waiting on someone or on everyone. Practice saying no, no, a thousand times no, at least twice a day, and you'll just barely have enough time to garden. I would be the first to concede that there's no way any of us can have a perfect garden. But trying to can be just as much fun as ocean racing, bird hunting, ice skating, or being president of the United States of America — and besides, you don't have to dress the part.

The reflecting pool is only one and a half inches deep, but absolutely flat so that the water evaporates evenly. A girl with a goose peers over the mound of ivy that repeats the curve.

Martha Adams

COLUMBIA, SOUTH CAROLINA

The nymph is a family heirloom from an old plantation garden. A hedge of cherry laurel screens the back of the yard from the neighbors.

I CAN'T IMAGINE life without my garden. It started for me with a grandmother who grew everything from camellias to cotton on a thirteen-acre farm and religiously ordered her seed the second week of each January. My memory holds the vision of spontaneous flower arrangements as only "Nan" could make, changing from the earliest pink camellias in January to the bright zinnias of July. My mother, Emily Whaley, raised in this delicious environment, had no choice but to go the gardening route. Although hers is a city garden, every time I visit it I see, to my delight, that the character and individuality of her country rearing has left its definite stamp. It's refreshing to see a garden unlike any other.

How could I, the granddaughter and daughter of these two creative gardeners, not put my hand to the trowel? The pleasure I get is equal to theirs, I promise you. Gardening really became part of me during a two-year stay (courtesy of the United States Air Force) in Southern California, where geraniums are shrubs and there is no frost. On our return to Columbia, we were ready to buy a house, and it never occurred to us not to make a lovely little garden on our new property.

To encourage this venture, my grandmother offered the services of Loutrell Briggs as the designer. This gift has continued to aid me for twelve years, and its benefits will go on and on. Mr. Briggs came up with the ideal plan of three rectangular compartments in our sixty-by-sixty-foot space after a fifteen-minute stroll around the plot. The following month we had a mason in for the terrace and brick coping. We learned bricklaying skills from him and laid all the paths and the summerhouse foundation ourselves. My back is still hurting a decade later, I'm sorry to report, but our paths are really lovely.

As the garden fits snugly into the elbow of our L-shaped house, it offers us lovely views from all our rooms. We have turned some downstairs windows into doors to give us quick access to our garden "room." Characteristic of Mr. Briggs's designs are garden compartments subtly offering surprise, a note of mystery, and a mood change within a very small space. The surprising feature in our garden is a long allée planted with evergreen holly ferns, hosta, Lenten roses, and a "wall" of loquat. This allée ends at the summerhouse foundation, which we will complete when time, energy, and funds permit. Another compartment is reached by a path covered by a charming arbor built by my husband from columns salvaged from an old house. And since the house is L-shaped, we see different views from the two wings, giving the feeling of two different gardens.

The lovely nymph who presides over the semicircle at the end of the formal garden was inherited from my great-aunt, who had placed her as the main focal point of the garden at Gypsy Plantation in the Carolina Low Country. A seasonal procession of flowers surrounds the statue, beginning with tulips and continuing with amaryllis, iris, pinks, Enchantment lilies, and ending in the fall with *Sedum spectabile* 'Autumn Joy'.

The garden is now ten years old, so it has become established enough to require hard pruning every spring to keep the woody material in scale. But I am always on the lookout for plants that can earn their way into my garden because they have foliar as well as flower interest; the oakleaf hydrangea is a good example. I'm exploring the many varieties of sedums, as these are drought-resistant candidates for my many pots and wall planters. My garden is different every year as I search out new possibilities.

This leads me to say that I am one of the few gardeners in my area who experiments and studies gardening in depth. As a result, I do a television spot in hope of reaching those who never considered gardening or think of it as a difficult or an esoteric hobby. The spot is catching on, I am happy to say, and I have made hundreds of new gardening friends — friends despite the fact that I make very opinionated statements about horrid azalea color combinations, the lack of pruning knowledge around town, and the apparent fear of planting anything but marigolds.

I now have a small son and daughter. The next gardening generation, they often join me as I sow seeds, they share in discussions on which climbing rose would look best against the brick walls, and they dine at our table ablossom with the changing hues and scents of our flowers.

The spring view changes from window to window. The birdhouse marks the path leading through the Carolina jasmine-clad walls to the loquat allée. A gate to the arbor opens from the right side of the yard.

THE GARDEN OF

Ruth Levitan

STAMFORD, CONNECTICUT

I N 1956 my husband and I bought a modest contemporary house on a sloping wooded acre in Stamford. A developer had carved lots out of old Connecticut farmland that had reverted to forest, and we chose our site for the lovely dogwood trees. It is a measure of both our enthusiasm and our ignorance that we envisioned a marvelous garden in the middle of the woods. We were so eager to get started that we drove out from Manhattan to plant spring bulbs while the house was still under construction.

While our three daughters were small our efforts were erratic and we made little progress in coping with nature. There were many trees with enormous root systems, the underbrush was tangled and thorny, and the soil seemed to be composed mainly of rocks. Ten years later Jim commented wryly that in only a decade we had transformed a little house in the woods into a little house in a small clearing in the woods.

A ruff of blue Jacob's ladder around a shrub bed of pieris, rhododendron, and a deep pink gable azalea 'Boudoir' at the back door. In the foreground, double early tulips interplanted with forget-me-nots.

The pool set in a spring glade of forget-me-nots, basket of gold (Alyssum saxatile) and 'Hino Crimson' azaleas.

Progress was also slow because we started small with our planting materials. "Dig some holes," Jim said one day, having sent away for six blue spruce. Obediently I prepared a substantial plot, only to find when the trees arrived that all six fit neatly into a bathroom glass. But we persisted. Bargain shrubs grew to blooming size. At the cost of considerable marital controversy a number of big trees came down. On countless occasions we returned from dinner with Jim's parents in Norwalk lugging a box of perennial divisions for the new sunny spaces or a tangle of ground cover to be separated and set out around the shrubs. And as the girls spent their days in school I was free to spend more time outside enjoying the rhythm of the seasons.

Each new phase of the garden grew from what was there before. The endless supply of rocks built walls and terraces. Wildlings and ferns were rescued from building sites nearby. The original contours of the land are basically unchanged and I risk divorce if I remove another tree. I find land rather like a person you marry thinking you can change him — and of course you can't. Essentially we still live in the woods, and once the leaves are out, every ray of sunshine is precious. And Connecticut is prone to summer droughts and we depend on a well, which

A medley of Phlox divaricata, Dicentra eximia, Alyssum saxatile, *Johnny jump up, ajuga, and pansies among azaleas and dogwood.*

limits our watering. Unlike my tennis-playing neighbors, I'm delighted when the forecast is for "rain all weekend."

An acre of ground provides the opportunity for a great deal of gardening if you don't dedicate a large sweep of it to lawn. Around a central garden in a fairly open, sunny space are winding grassy paths bordered with spring-flowering plants and shrubs. These provide a transition between the intensely cultivated area and the surrounding woods. There are vistas that give a sense of discovery and benches for moments of quiet contemplation. Although I am now the principal gardener, Jim is still my best audience. We tour the grounds together all year round, often with wineglasses in hand, admiring fresh handiwork or a newly opened blossom, planning for the future or checking on the depredations of our many natural enemies.

After a visit to the Alhambra I was convinced that no garden could be complete without running water and began an ambitious excavation between two centrally located boulders. This was one do-it-yourself project that was beyond us and for once we ended up hiring workmen to finish digging and pouring cement. Now there is a little fishpond with a fountain and water lilies.

Wishing to learn more about the plants I had come to enjoy so much, I enrolled in a wonderful series of horticultural courses at the New York Botanical Garden. In honor of my Certificate in Botany and in celebration of our twenty-fifth wedding anniversary we contracted for a lean-to greenhouse. After all the years of starting seedlings under growlights among the wet towels in the laundry area, it was a delight to have the proper facilities. Jim forces bulbs, and I concentrate on plants like snapdragons, cinerarias, and primulas that provide lots of winter color and can then be jettisoned while I tend the seedlings in the spring and move outside in the summer.

Perhaps it is all those years of school openings, but to me fall still seems the year's real beginning, which indeed it must be if the spring is to be all you desire. There is never enough time in the fall for all the new projects as well as for the division of the perennials and the planting of bulbs. For me, planting a bulb is like mailing yourself a special surprise present. As the days shorten, I treasure every hour outdoors and am busy raking, clipping, and putting the garden tidily to bed for the winter. I'm also likely to cruise around town in my station wagon collecting bagged leaves left at curbside, bringing them back to my compost pile.

Spring is our loveliest time. What is more enchanting than finding crocus and aconite suddenly on display in a protected spot one early March morning? There is an almost fairyland quality to April and May as forsythia, andromeda, magnolias, dogwoods, and azaleas bloom in sequence above a Persian carpet of daffodils, tulips, and scilla interspersed with wild *Phlox divaricata,* Jacob's ladder, and other old-fashioned perennials. Later in the season ferns dominate the wild-flower paths among the flowering shrubs, since annuals are too greedy to trust there.

We look to the central garden for color in July and August when the warm hues of lilies and daylilies contrast with the cool blues of hostas (their foliage hides the dying daffodil leaves), baptisia and echinops. Hydrangeas, snowball

An undulating border of (from front to back) Johnny jump up, candytuft, Phlox divaricata, *Jacob's ladder, and ajuga.*

bushes, and rose-of-Sharon provide a backdrop. Shade tolerant annuals like impatiens and nicotiana surround the pool, while several varieties of sedum form colonies that cling to the exposed roots of the beech tree.

Of course I keep a diary. Part of the fun of gardening is looking back and comparing "then" and "now." But I did overhear one daughter telling another: "Want to read something boring? Sneak a look at mother's diary — all about the weather." Although the diary is a reminder for chores, I also have a personal timetable. I like to clip pussy willow and forsythia for indoor forcing on our wedding anniversary — January 30; to have all the seedlings out of the greenhouse by Memorial Day; to have all of the bulbs in the ground by Halloween, and the compost piles built by Thanksgiving.

While the girls were young they were totally uninterested in helping with the garden. In fact they felt unfortunate to have a mother who was reluctant to wash up and change her clothes to drive to Girl Scouts or go shopping. Occasionally a teenager on a diet would volunteer to mow the lawn "for exercise." Still later they enjoyed showing the garden off to friends and wanted garden weddings. Now they are all married with homes of their own and the oldest and youngest are enthusiastic gardeners. We enjoy working outside together when I visit them. Our middle daughter is very much a city girl and still hates to get her fingernails dirty.

Our rocky garden has become my art form and one that is never static. Fortunately a plant is not like a child or a pet. Malingerers can be trundled off to the mulch pile. And I can try to be philosophical when a special favorite is trampled by a dog, chewed by raccoons, excavated by skunks, or demolished by slugs. There are always fresh seeds to order and new methods to explore. My attitude is that if at first you don't succeed, try, try again; but try something different!

My parents were idealists. Now nearly sixty, I still believe what they taught me as a child — that life's highest goal is the making of a better world for all, one with peace, justice, freedom, and equality. I've spent countless hours standing on vigils, organizing petition drives, going to meetings. The long days gardening in the solitude of the out of doors have always been a necessary balance to the excitement and frustration of the political arena.

In a way gardening carried on another family tradition. My mother cared passionately about the beauty of the natural world although she never made a garden as such. Among my earliest and most precious memories are walks with her learning the names of the wild flowers and the native trees. She would call my sister and me from our studies to share a rainbow, a sunset or a starry sky. As the years pass and our unique planet is increasingly threatened by the destructiveness of mankind, my garden has come to be my reassurance as well as my retreat. The incredible capacity of living things to survive, the infinite resourcefulness of nature — is this not a good omen for us all?

Primroses add a deep hue to the rainbow of spring color.

Eleanor Perényi

COASTAL CONNECTICUT

OR CLOSE on thirty years, I have gardened on a bit less than an acre of New England village ground and been happy with the results, because, though too formally divided into parts to be called a cottage garden, it resembles one in having a little of everything: a section for vegetables and small fruits and another for roses, with a grape arbor running between them; a herb bed; a lawn almost if not quite fit to be called a croquet pitch; and last but not least four large island beds filled with perennials, which if viewed from a slight distance might be mistaken for English herbaceous borders. Nothing was perfect, but all of it good enough. Or so I thought until I got the idea of writing a book about gardening, and almost from the hour of the publication of *Green Thoughts* I have been in trouble. No longer do I scan my efforts with the indulgent eye of the anonymous amateur. I see faults wherever I look, and the reason is that in some subtle way it has ceased to be altogether mine. People have read about it, and having read about it, quite a few

Daylilies along the lattice fence that divides the vegetable garden from the lawn and flower garden.

want to see it — imagining, no doubt, that it must be original in design, surely will contain interesting if not rare plants, and at the very least be an example of how a proud gardener maintains a property.

The truth, of course, is otherwise — as I now see all too plainly when I wander about asking myself such questions as why I have tolerated the banality of a grape arbor all these years, why I haven't managed even the tiniest *pièce d'eau* to reflect the sky, and for the thousandth time how I am to rid the lawn of ground ivy. In other words, I have begun to see the garden less as a private preserve where I muddle through with varying degrees of success than as a sort of showplace fit for public display. And that, as I also see, is a disastrous mistake. The garden is what it is and will never be very different. Not for me a consultation with an eminent designer like Russell Page; nor am I likely at this late date to join the ranks of those who devote their lives to the study and care of unusual plants. I dream of such luxuries — what gardener doesn't? — but in practice would settle for an intelligent helper willing to turn up a couple of times a week for a sum I could afford.

Balloon flowers and lilies in the flower garden near the house. The weeping beech at the left marks the boundary with the churchyard.

Lacecap hydrangeas by the summer house.

The Old Congregational church beyond the rose garden and grape arbor.

The view from the church steeple: the vegetable garden is in the center foreground; the grape arbor beyond separates it from the rose garden. The flower garden is to the right, hidden by trees.

In the meantime, the garden is — dare I say? — perhaps not so bad after all. It produces, for one thing, a bountiful harvest of flowers for the house, vegetables and fruit for the table; and for another is an inexhaustible source of pleasure and puzzlement — for example, those Madonna lilies, planted years ago and long since forgotten because they did so poorly, which have suddenly rejuvenated themselves and bloomed furiously in one corner of a perennial bed. A garden like mine can make up for what it lacks in elegance and planning with an abundance of little mysteries like this one, and for a gardener like me they must suffice.

Sarah & Virginia Weatherly

KANSAS CITY, MISSOURI

Cucumber and Israeli melon vines scramble around young tomato plants in supporting cages. Seedling carrots, pattypan squash, and beets appear in the central panel.

MOVING to this pocket-size city garden in 1943 was a great challenge to our mother, a self-taught horticulturist. The quarter-acre lot was less than half the size of our grandparents' garden in Hannibal, without counting their tennis court and upper vegetable garden. It was shady and the soil seemed to be mostly cinders and bottle caps. This was a new kind of gardening and necessitated much research among the works of mother's "oracles" — Helen Van Pelt Wilson, Richardson Wright, Montague Free, and Gertrude Jekyll. The Kansas City "shirtwaist" house (half stone and half frame) was comfortable and available in those war years, but the eye needed to be distracted from its ugliness.

Our mother planted hemlocks and yews to screen the front of the house and she made a flowering shrubbery on the far side of the driveway at the back of the lot. Liberal additions of manure, available from cattle-loading stations along the railroad, helped to improve the soil. That manure was very different from today's weed-free variety, as we remember all too well.

On the windiest of March days, our mother asked us to lay out her Sweet Herb Garden. The plan was one she had found in some book of Charleston gardens and drawn on a slip of paper hoping one day to use it. Now she had made full-sized patterns of the twelve beds on heavy craft paper. Until the outline could be traced, every available brick, tool, and heavy object was used to hold these patterns in place. Needless to say, tempers were short before the job was done. Now the beds hold yellow basket of gold (*Alyssum saxatile compactum*), a welcome sight here in the spring along with miniature daffodils. Later pink flowering *Geranium lancastrense* (or as we love to call it, Pretty Polly) fill the four cloverleaf beds surrounding an ivy-covered pedestal holding a stone basket of flowers. Two beds of blue catmint (*Nepeta mussinii*) bloom with the geraniums, as do Sweet Williams (*Dianthus barbatus* 'Newport Pink'), the dwarf gray-leaved *Achillea taygetea*, and deep blue *Salvia* 'East Friesland'.

We must sound very grand in referring to our Sweet Herb Garden, Grass Walk, Vegetable Garden, Perennial Garden, Culinary Herb Bed, Daylily Bed, Shrubbery Border, and Old Rose Hedge. In fact we garden in two areas of only about forty by eighty feet each on the east and west sides of the house and in a space of twenty-five by forty feet at the back. This rear area holds the Sweet Herb

and the Vegetable Gardens. Although we cannot have mass plantings, we have tried valiantly to cultivate every square inch of the property. We have even relegated some favorite "spreading herbs" like tansy and *Artemisia* 'Silver King' to the strip between the sidewalk and the street.

It is surely a universal experience that changes in circumstances necessitate changes in gardens. In the Grass Walk, the original shade-loving plants are gone since six giant American elms succumbed to disease. When our six-foot euonymus hedge was winter-killed in 1981–82, we had to erect a cedar fence to protect the plants from the northwest winter wind and our ears from the street noises. Many clematis now climb this fence. These changes gave us some exciting vacant soil. Since we had been enjoying the fruit from a five-year-old dwarf cherry tree, we could hardly wait to plant our additional "orchard" in the new space. (We are amused by the incredulous expressions on faces when we now refer to our orchard — two dwarf apple trees and three dwarf peaches.) Then *our* "oracle," Rachel Snyder, editor of *Flower and Garden* magazine, remarked that this area could accommodate Exbury azaleas. Enthusiastically we made six half-circles in the grass, and now these deciduous and fragrant azaleas alternate with the fruit trees.

Fragrance is very important to us and we enjoy the early scents of *Viburnum carlesii*, *Narcissus* 'Trevithian,' and Missouri currant. Then come the Exburys and dwarf Korean lilacs, followed by mock orange, lavender, and old roses. The Carolina sweet shrub (*Calycanthus floridus*) by the front door provides a delightful strawberry fragrance in June from its chocolate-brown flowers, which are shaped like unopened rosebuds. Its wood is even more fragrant than its flowers, making pruning an agreeable chore. The witch hazel on the other side of the front door (*Hamamelis virginiana*) blooms in October and November, supplying pungently scented yellow pinwheel blossoms for Thanksgiving.

Old-fashioned roses form a hedge along the east side of the lot and a background for our Perennial Garden of geometric raised beds. We have only one hybrid tea rose, 'Dainty Bess', which sits in haughty grandeur in a small circular raised bed surrounded by lavender Hidcote and Vera. The lavender has seeded in the foundation sand of the brick paths. As these seedlings are not as deep a color as Hidcote but darker than the Vera, we laughingly refer to them as "Weatherly Hybrids." The rest of our roses are the intensely fragrant old varieties purchased from Bobbink & Atkins forty years ago — Moss, Cabbage, Damask, and three Pillars. The underplantings are wild ginger and showy primroses.

All our perennials are grown in raised beds — as the result of an accident. One night two sturdy boys toppled a decorative open-work brick wall (obviously not as sturdy as the boys). We had already been interested in using raised beds, and after laboriously chipping away the mortar from the fallen bricks we used them to construct the beds. This has been very satisfactory, as the garden is on the down slope and now the drainage is much better. Mosses grow in the old pink brick paths. Among our most rewarding perennials are veronicas and campanulas.

The annuals are started in January and germinate well under growlights: French marigolds (we were always told they deterred nematodes), nicotianas,

The foliage of Geranium lancastriense, *nepeta, and liriope in the sweet herb garden in late summer. Thymes grow among the bricks of the path.*

A golden rain tree shades the brick terrace and shelters a thirty-year-old bay tree and other houseplants.

'Hidcote' and 'Vera' lavenders bloom in
the circular center bed of the perennial
garden. Flowering behind the clipped
Korean box hedge are sulfur-colored
Achillea taggetea, lythrum 'Morden's
Pink', and Allium albopilosum. Old
French roses line the fence, with the
daylily bed beyond.

ornamental peppers, love-in-a-mist, and our favorite, dianthus. We also start delphiniums and treat them as biennials. There is always something new to try.

A narrow bed filled with culinary herbs divides the garden from the terrace.
We have copied a medieval garden feature here and planted a seat of thyme where
you can sit on a fragrant "cushion" of this herb. The brick terrace is shaded by a
golden rain tree and edged with fraises des bois. A five-foot bay tree, which winters
in the garage, and the houseplants are very happy under this light shade. Opposite
the terrace and extending the rose hedge is a daylily bed with some forty varieties.
This is our one big splash of color.

In the front, along with evergreens, our color comes from *Kolkwitzia amabilis*,
underplanted with Kaufmannia tulips, and *Cornus florida* 'White Cloud', with early
spring bulbs coming through ajuga and the whole underplanting encircled with
liriope. Against the only surviving part of our tall euonymus hedge fairy roses are
interplanted with self-seeding feverfew. Ferns have a happy home under *Hamamelis
virginiana* and some are so exuberant they encroach into the lawn.

The Shrubbery Border on the back of the property is the original planting,
with the exception of a variegated Cornelian cherry espaliered against the cedar-
wood fence. Here are Korean lilac, Philadelphus, abelia, *Deutzia lemoinei* (why is

this lovely shrub no longer offered?), *Viburnum carlesii*, *Clematis davidiana*, *Hypericum* 'Hidcote', *Deutzia gracilis*, pyracantha, and flowering almond. The underplanting is of several colors of our Missouri wild geranium and *Geranium sanguineum*. When the coral bells became unhappy in the Sweet Herb Garden, we moved them to this border and they have flourished.

Our pride and joy is the twelve-by-twenty-foot Vegetable Garden. We have a rotation of crops, which supplies our table and even some produce for our sister and our dinner parties. Beginning with Sugar Snap peas, we harvest a dozen vegetables. This year we experimented with dwarf broccoli and Israeli hybrid melons. Climbing nasturtiums usurped the fence from cucumbers, which seem to prefer their tepee stakes.

Even before we both retired, the two of us did all the work. We had taken over most of the responsibility from Mother about five years before her death in 1962. We even did all the brick work, but that was fifteen to thirty years ago and then the job was easier. We often hear remarks like, "But it is so much work," or "You must spend all your time in the garden." Our only response is that it has not been work but pleasure to us, and we wish only we had more time for it.

Ann E. McPhail

PHILADELPHIA, PENNSYLVANIA

THE JOYS AND CHALLENGES associated with a city garden are endless. When my husband and I moved back into Philadelphia twenty years ago we chose to rent for a while. I gained valuable experience working with two quite different gardens, varying in size and exposure. One might wonder why I needed more experience after attending years of intensive classes in horticulture at the Barnes Foundation Arboretum in Merion, Pennsylvania. In fact, the normal teaching approach to horticulture is based on ideal conditions and garden practices, while I found that city space and climatic conditions are often far from normal.

In 1968 we acquired a property which comprised four house lots, one with a long, rambling house built around 1850. Our first view of the property was dismal, since for several years the house had been unoccupied above the first floor. The land surrounding it, used as a parking lot, was completely sterile from years of dumping cinders from the ancient coal furnace in the cellar. The one point in favor of buying was the anticipation of a large (for a city) garden area. Friends gave no encouragement, but we went ahead.

After renovations on the house were accomplished, I began landscaping the garden by drawing up a scaled plan, and I have adhered to this basically ever since. The plan anticipated a pavilion sitting area, a serpentine bed along the left boundary wall, and cold frames and plantings behind a low retaining wall at the far left-hand corner. Two pools were included, and I planned a large island bed for taller trees and shrubs.

As the whole garden would be public to high-rise buildings and nearby row houses, the layout emphasized privacy. And while there is always an undercurrent of traffic noise in any city, our plant material now acts as a baffle to reduce sound.

When new masonry walls were built around the perimeter, the workmen excavating the footings uncovered an abundance of beautiful gray Pennsylvania fieldstone, used in earlier times in wall constructions. These stones played an important role in the designs I made later, used as various edgings, additions to the pebble walkways of my herb garden, and the serpentine wall.

I had to wait three years before starting the construction of the garden, and my first project was the herb area. This has a distinct Japanese feeling, as stepping stones are set with pebbles and smooth round stones collected from the rivers in

Saponaria, strawberry begonias, Phlox subulata, and hardy geraniums in bloom along the wall. A collection of dwarf ivies edge the pool at left and form a natural barrier against fishing cats.

October reveals the architecture of the garden, including the forms of the weeping autumn cherry, the 'Dorothea' crab in the island bed, and the European river birches along the wall. The herb garden is seen between the house and the pavilion.

A succession of bulbs and perennials add color to a collection of conifers and evergreens. In bloom at the same time as the crab are bleeding heart, tulips, narcissus, candytuft, Phlox subulata, *and Jacob's ladder.*

Maine. To simulate moss, which will not survive our summer sun, various mat-forming thymes were used, including *Thymus serpyllum* and *T. serpyllum languinosus.* The garden is backed by bamboos in a cement trough and espaliered hardy orange (*Poncirus trifoliata*). Bamboo is beautiful but it must be confined, for with a system of underground rhizomes it has a secret and rampant growth habit.

I find the soft grays and blue greens of the herbs especially attractive; I love trimming them — their scent is marvelous. I use fresh herbs in salads, sorrel for soup, and fennel for fish. Each August I pick the huge fennel plume, dry it briefly, and take it to northern Maine to friends who run a French restaurant there; they find it is not hardy that far north. In the fall I dry and freeze many herbs for winter use. The large rosemary bushes, the Greek bay plant, and scented geraniums are potted and kept in the basement artificial light unit.

The use of oriental touches in my garden grows out of other personal interests. For years I have lectured on a variety of oriental subjects at the Philadelphia Museum of Art, and I have studied Chinese brush painting, so many of the plants in our garden relate to subjects in Chinese paintings.

I had to wait five years before funds were available to build the pavilion. It has three sides, with a wide, slightly sloping lower roof covering a sitting and eating–entertaining area. Underneath the pavilion I store everything from ladders to insecticides. Twenty years ago I grew a holly, *Ilex aquifolium,* from seed, and this has come with me through each successive move; it now shades the pavilion. For the last six years it has borne berries, but I have no idea where the male holly is! It is underplanted with ferns and in contrast nearby are several Japanese maples.

Now that you have an idea of the design of the garden, I want to tell you a bit about the plants I have used. At the far end of the serpentine wall we planted an Atlas cedar trained to grow horizontally; how else could a small garden accommodate a tree with a growth potential of 120 feet? Along the wall are espaliered evergreen euonymus, cotoneasters, birch, pieris, all with underplanting of prostrate junipers and hardy perennials such as hostas and geraniums. At the lower level, in front of the wall, Hinoki cypress, heathers, armeria, iberis, and ivies all fit into its curves. Here two pools are designed to over-winter goldfish, reeds, and swamp iris. A pebble walk partially surrounds the pools — very practical, as this provides drainage for the lowest point in the garden.

The planting bed by the house is designed as a free-form island surrounded by brick and pebbled paths. A crab shelters the French holly, the fragrant snowball viburnum (*V. carlacelphalum*), azaleas, and the dwarf pink rhododendron 'Beaufort' underplanted with liriopes and ivies. Near the house you should grow your favorite plants. I love *Prunus subhirtella* 'Pendula' for autumn and winter form. In the summer, from the greenhouse on the third floor and the light unit in the basement come camellias, fig, a loquat, and big and little pittosporums. I can make endless combinations of aristocratic plants here.

The upkeep of the garden has to be systemized or I would be working at it all and every day. I usually spend an hour before dinner several days a week and water early in the morning in summer. Every other weekend I like to spend one whole day pruning, spraying for insects, and doing many other routine jobs. I

In front of the lavender in the center of the herb garden are santolina, mother of thyme, and woodruff. Espaliered on the wall are ivy, variegated euonymus, poncirus, and evergreen euonymus. A collection of thymes creeps among the stones.

tried a new drip watering system this summer, and I think, with some adjustments, the system will work in many areas in the garden. My life-style does not allow me to spend as much time as I really should in my garden, as it remains a high maintenance one, with much plant material squeezed in.

Plants in a city garden are always under unusual stress. The surrounding buildings can cause sudden heating up or cooling down. A shadow suddenly passes and the full intensity of the sun hits a bed, and just as suddenly another angle shadow falls on a hot area and it cools down too quickly. There are few gradual transitions in a city garden.

Yet the garden remains beautiful all the year round, and the gardener's critical eye is tempered by the excitement of seasonal renewal and changes. There is charm from the first snowdrops shivering in the cold of late winter to that warm day in late April when a ragged flock of returning fish crows wheel by in search of their old home in a nearby watertank, and announce that summer is coming to all in Philadelphia. The hot summer and glorious autumn give way to winter, when the crabapples turn yellow, holly berries are red, and the junipers along the stone wall turn a beautiful purple blue. Every season has its mood and coloration, its joys and challenges.

Helen Smith

COLORADO SPRINGS, COLORADO

Rain! A soft gentle rain was falling when we left the house of a
friend the other evening and I knew it meant I would not have
to water the garden tomorrow. My life is dictated by water, as it
becomes the overriding concern all summer. A traditional garden
here can be maintained only by irrigation or sprinkling. Thirty-
five years ago when I made it, there was no pressure to conserve water.

An iris catalogue sent me down the flowering path I have taken all these
years. I had to have some of these beautiful flowers in my new garden. We were
moving into a Victorian-era house in the oldest part of the city and it seemed
appropriate to have an English perennial garden because the city was founded and
planned by an Englishman. And by good chance I found a talented English
landscape architect, Katherine Marriage, who designed the perennial garden and
guided the addition of new shrubs. She found that the already established border
of Persian lilac along the west boundary was just what she liked as a background
for the border. To my astonishment no iris were in her plan. I had not mentioned
the iris catalogue, the inspiration for it all. Iris, of course, were added. When
spring came my husband and I began planting, often with no knowledge of the
plants we were placing. We have been changing and extending ever since.

It wasn't until the second year of the garden that I realized we had made a
color-coordinated garden, a miracle to us. The spring colors, just before and during
the time of lilac bloom, are lavender, blue, and yellow. The next period is one of
many hues, with iris, peonies, lupines, and dictamnus grouped for harmonizing
color and texture. Later in the summer the colors are white, blue, pink, and red.
August and September bring in the yellows and reds, with more blue, of course.

Ever since I have been adding new plants to intensify the color display,
especially when the original plantings were small and there was plenty of room.
It was easy to see that aubrietia, violets, yellow daffodils, purple and yellow tulips,
doronicum, and brunnera would add charm to the spring array. June is a rainbow
of iris. The great assets of July and August are astilbes and thalictrums in the
shady areas, and campanulas, true geraniums, and veronicas in the sunny ones. I
am still looking for a daylily to match the red of my Leo Schlageter phlox or one
of the perfect shade of apple blossom pink. The addition of various species of
goldenrod and dwarf asters and tall cimicifugas has been my only contribution to

A charming mix of tall bearded iris, lupine, dictamnus, and alliums against the Persian lilac hedge in late May.

A branch of a sunburst locust tree in the foreground, silhouetted against an American elm in the center of the yard. By the house are the new terraced beds with young Picea glauca albertiana conica, Cotinus coggygria atropurpurea, *and* Amelanchier canadensis *treated as shrubs.*

the fall flowers in the original plan, which called for heleniums and Michaelmas daisies. I am always fighting the battle for the use of our native goldenrods. No other garden perennial has its grace and the Arnold Arboretum is my authority for believing its pollen does not cause hay fever.

Iris catalogues continue to be an annual temptation and I try to refine our collection in the color ranges I prefer. In the blue-purple group 'First Violet' is a fine old variety and I've been very pleased with the new 'Mystique', a 1980 Dykes Medal winner that has standards of light violet and violet-purple falls. Another old favorite belongs in the yellow group, 'Apricot Glory', while a recent addition is 'Old Flame', which has perfect form and is white with a narrow border of gold and a bright red beard. A delightful new pink is 'Peach Frost' with color shading from peach to pink and a tangerine beard.

Getting the exact color I want is always a problem and I feel strongly that all nurseries and catalogues should use the Royal Horticultural color charts for truly accurate color description.

Over the years maturing trees cast more and more shade, making the perennials grow too tall and less sturdy. We do have almost full sun at the front of our house and there we have plantings only four years old. They were inspired by the installation of a wonderful old wrought-iron fence which we first admired and photographed beside a house in Florence, Colorado. One day the woman who lived there was in her yard and we stopped and chatted. We got to know her, and when she decided to move we persuaded her to sell us the fence. Then we removed the old juniper "foundation" plantings from the front of the house and built up a series of terraces retained by flat low stone walls. This has become a green garden of marvelous shapes and textures of foliage. Only a few white tulips, daffodils, two yellow iris, and some *Alyssum saxatile,* white arenaria, and yellow lilies indicate seasonal change.

We have acquired a fine library of garden books, including a treasured copy of *The Genus Iris* by W. R. Dykes in the 1913 original edition, a gift from Katherine Marriage. But it is really from traveling that we gain much of our information. And this is how we have found our most interesting plants. We go yearly to the Colonial Williamsburg Garden Symposium and to many of the American Horticultural Society meetings and tours. We discovered tree peonies on Cape Cod and now have eight of these elegant beauties in our sunny northwest corner. 'Gauguin', with its yellow color shaded with orange-apricot tones, is especially lovely. Our fraises des bois, 'Catherine the Great', are the border planting for the collection.

Blue Haven junipers in a special niche in the perennial border form a backdrop for Campanula percisifolia alba *and three kinds of astilbes.*

In Amsterdam at the 1971 Floriade we saw dwarf conifers for the first time and have since traveled to the Arnold Arboretum and the National Arboretum in Washington, D.C. to learn more about them. We have become adept at packing these superb little trees and bringing them home from East Coast nurseries because no nursery in our area carries more than three or four kinds. With about forty scattered over our yard we probably have the best collection in the state. About twenty of them are planted in the front terraces and we put up miniature picket fences to protect them from scorching in the bright winter sun. Visitors rarely notice these little treasures because of their unfamiliarity, but on any day I can admire their finely textured foliage and go and ruffle my hands through the little 'Kammies' with the greatest of pleasure. The silvery blue-gray of *Chamaecyparis pisifera* 'Boulevard' especially delights me since its color is so similar to that of the 'Blue Haven' juniper. Our real baby is a five-inch *Pinus strobus* 'Witches Broom', a gift from Peter Del Tredici of the Arnold Arboretum. In a country where blue spruce is native and common but its dwarfs are not, I am happy to have finally succeeded in buying the dwarf *Picea pungens* 'R. H. Montgomery', which has pendulous foliage.

Our collection of euonymus is also unusual in Colorado. The first were planted at the suggestion of Mrs. Marriage and we have added more. They do well in the shade and the fall color of some is appreciated. Perhaps the most admired feature of the yard is the *Euonymus fortunei radicans vegetatus* espaliered on the south wall under the elm tree.

I find pleasure in replanting and redesigning small areas, one at a time. There is always the excitement of replacing old varieties with better new hybrids. There is also pleasure in good grooming. There can be no successful garden without it. With a fine tool, pruning is irresistible. There is no time to allow either the garden or myself to grow old. And I shall continue to water it all.

The prized wrought-iron fence silhouetted against the fall color of Euonymus alatus compactus.

THE GARDEN OF

Pamela Copeland

MOUNT CUBA,
GREENVILLE, DELAWARE

*Yellow lady's slipper (*Cyprepedium pubescens).

The margins of a woodland pond offer an ideal environment for Primula japonica *and* Phlox stononifera alba.

I BELIEVE MY LOVE of gardens and flowers came from my mother, whom I would accompany as a child as she walked around her gardens in Connecticut consulting with the Scots head gardener, who always worked in a shirt, tie, dark suit, bowler hat and a green canvas apron. Above all I looked forward to our walks across the pastures behind our house and along the river to the woods beyond. Mother taught me to look for nature's flowers and later encouraged my interest with prizes for wildflower collections labeled with both the common and Latin names and the families to which they belonged.

Although for a few years my interest in men overcame my interest in plants, as soon as I married the need for flowers revived my enthusiasm, and they became as important as the new duties I was learning as a housewife. My first garden was a small border of annuals for cut flowers and lettuce and parsley.

In 1935 my husband's business brought us to Delaware, which had always been his home, and we set about looking for land. Being a New Englander, I felt I must have a hill. We found Mount Cuba and built our house on the crest of the hill overlooking a vista of rolling fields of corn and stands of native deciduous trees, mostly tulip poplar (*Liriodendron tulipifera*). We did little formal landscaping until after World War II, except for screen plantings of white pines and hemlocks. There are still extensive acres that have not been disturbed for at least fifty years where colonies of Dutchman's breeches (*Dicentra cucullaria*), bloodroot (*Sanguinaria canadensis*), and rue-anemone (*Anemonella thalictroides*) and other early spring wildflowers flourish in the shade of oaks, hickories, walnuts, and American beech.

When we were ready to begin the formal gardens, Henry Francis du Pont recommended Marian Coffin as the very best and most imaginative landscape architect. She had worked with Mr. du Pont at Winterthur, so we were able to judge her work. I found her delightful and liked her concept of big sweeps of a single plant in variations of a single color range. In this manner she created for us long azalea borders in a rectangular walled garden where Ghent and Mollis azaleas begin near the house with yellows, progress through the oranges, and end at the entrance to the round garden in reds and bronzes. Unclipped billowing boxwood surrounds the round garden and is punctuated at regular intervals by four pyra-

midal American hollies (*Ilex opaca*). The pool in the center, deep enough for swimming, represents the cavetto of a plate, with the border formed by four flower beds which change with the seasons.

In the early sixties, the focus of my gardening changed when we were able to purchase an adjacent meadow and woodlot near our entrance drive. I had seen many native wildlings in areas quite distant from the house, but here was an opportunity to develop a naturalistic garden that was more readily accessible. The land was wooded with majestic tulip poplars and screened from the house by our earlier planting of evergreen trees, rhododendrons, and azaleas. We cleared some glades in these woodlands and created ponds so there would be a place for plants that needed wet feet. I continued to follow Marian Coffin's concept of sweeps of individual varieties of plant material and it has worked well, with colonies of

Lavender Rhododendron mucronatum amethystinum *in the rectangular walled garden seen from the house terrace.*

ESTATE GARDENS

foamflower (*Tiarella cordifolia*), bleeding heart (*Dicentra eximia*), hepatica (*Hepatica americana*). So far, trailing arbutus (*Epigea repens*) and wintergreen (*Gaultheria procumbens*) have proven most temperamental.

Another plant that I have found hard to keep, as have other growers, is the lady's slipper. In some places they have done well and increased, but in others they have languished for a few years and ultimately died. This is partly due to their particular mycorrhizal requirements. Delaware has many threatened native lady's slippers. A farmer's field nearby is carpeted with them, but he has just sold the land for development and we are involved in the tricky task of transplanting them here. One of the challenges of wildflower cultivation is that the plants won't always stay where planted if they don't like the location. They die or the healthier ones move on to a place of their own choosing — sometimes not at all the place you want them, but such individualism helps make a contrived naturalistic garden more natural.

For background and boundary definition I've used native shrubs and taller plants such as *Ilex glabra, Ilex verticilla, Cornus alba sibirica, Cornus stolonifera,* and *Cornus stolonifera lutea* ('Flaviramea'), goatsbeard (*Aruncus dioicus*), blue cohosh (*Caulophyllum thalictroides*), and both snakeroots (*Cimicifuga racemosa* and *C. americana*). The native *Rhododendron prunifolium* gives a spectacular showing in July/August with its orange-red flowers and again in autumn, as its foliage is brilliant. In late summer the cardinal flower (*Lobelia cardinalis*) gives a fine splash of color along the rills and ponds.

I am trying many different plants as ground covers, as I dislike everything being one height. I am encouraging the use of our native pachysandra (*P. procumbens*), although it does not have the glossiness of the Japanese variety. And I use

The swimming pool designed by the noted American landscape architect Marian Coffin is the centerpiece of the round garden.

The gazebo in the woodland garden with dogwood.

wild bleeding heart, partridgeberry (*Mitchella repens*), *Shortia galacifolia*, and foam-flower. Yellowroot (*Xanthorhiza simplicissima*) is excellent as a rough, woody ground cover. A "foreign" ground cover that has proven useful in holding back the invasive honeysuckle after it has been (apparently) grubbed out is variegated goutweed (*Lamium galeobdolon*), but in time I may find it too intrusive.

As I became more deeply involved in the growing of wild plants, I became aware of the fact that nurseries sold material plundered from the woods in their areas to fill the increasing demand of home owners who believe the fantasy that a "wild" flower once planted fends for itself. This, plus the steady attrition of designated Delaware wildlands, opened my eyes to the need of conserving land for wildflowers to grow before they all became endangered species.

Up to that point my naturalistic garden had evolved very informally under my direction. Now, I wanted to become a serious, informed conservationist. With this in mind, I consulted Dr. Richard Lightly, who was at the time Coordinator of the Longwood Program. He expressed interest in my ideas and suggested enlarging the scope of my concerns from native Delaware flora exclusively to that of the whole Piedmont region. Our talks continued, and, happily for me, Dr.

The path to the gazebo with Phlox divaricata *and* Primula polyantha.

Lightly has become the first director of the Mount Cuba Center for the Study of Piedmont Flora, of which there are some 300 species. We are already experimenting with a computer that produces a topographic map of the property with a grid overlay. The location of each planting can be entered together with data about the microclimate. Then the effect of various sites and cultural practices on the same species can be compared. On my death the entire property will be open to the public. I hope to foster an appreciation of the beauty and diversity of wildflowers through display and education here at Mount Cuba, and to encourage people to become their conservators, guarding against the plundering of our few remaining wild lands.

Ruth Field

A LOW COUNTRY PLANTATION, SOUTH CAROLINA

Azaleas edge a path through one of the many collections of camellias scattered around the plantation.

THIS PLANTATION was originally a minor part of the Heyward family holdings in the Carolinas. They were one of the wealthiest of the Colonial and antebellum families, including among their members Thomas Heyward, a signer of the Declaration of Independence. Like many of the plantations in the area that had produced cotton and rice before the Civil War, it became a quail shooting property for new northern owners in the postwar era. And it was for its good natural shooting land that we came here and built our house in 1937. In those days the tenant farmers worked without modern machinery and often left natural patches that gave the quails food and shelter. Since farming here has become more professional we have had to put in some plantings for the birds. But they are still attracted by the acorns from the multitudes of live oaks.

Soon after our arrival we learned that the well-known garden designer Umberto Innocenti was doing work near by. My husband offered to engage him to lay out our plantings, but I thought it would be more fun to work out my own ideas. I don't, however, consider myself a serious gardener and really have just tried to enhance the natural features of the landscape. There is a natural allée of trees in the back garden, which we have accentuated, and there wisteria, which grows like a weed here, drapes over all the trees, creating a spectacular spring show.

The garden is really a series of allées and paths that lead to the camellia and rose gardens, the marsh, the tennis courts, or to a few formal brick-paved gardens with benches and statuary. Bloom starts here in January with masses of naturalized bulbs. Camellias are apt to be at their height in February. But the peak of color comes about the first week of April from the azaleas scattered among the live oaks, massed on the margins of the streams and the pond, and lined along the paths.

I have been surprisingly successful with rhododendrons here, especially with varieties that I brought down from my Long Island garden. But the real gardening adventures have come with camellias. When we first came here I worked with Mr. Prevatt, a respected local camellia judge, to upgrade the varieties of camellias on the plantation. He was a nurseryman by profession and worked for me on a retainer until I had my own gardener. He came once a week but always disappeared

Live oaks and limber pines reflected in a pond made by damming one of the creeks. Azaleas in the distance create a focal point.

for the three weeks around Christmas when he said so many people came along wanting camellias that the only thing he could do was lock his gate and go fishing.

The great immersion in camellias came after I engaged my longtime superintendent, now retired, whom I will just call Mr. A. Mr. A. had failed at running a nursery before coming here, but he never lost his determination to produce as many plants as possible. He kept growing seedling camellias and I kept having to find places to put them. We even built bridges across streams to get to new planting areas. I finally felt I had to ask him to try to practice plant birth control. He thought about it for a few days and then came and told me he couldn't; it was against his nature. He wouldn't even prune the camellias, so I had to do it. He grafted masses of 'Betty Sheffield', a medium pink camellia, so we have a whole glade of them. Fortunately he liked one of my favorites, the old double white 'Alba plena', a very early bloomer. But after Mr. A. produced his own registered camellia variety, my life wasn't worth living. He wouldn't look at any other kind. And even though he named it after one of my daughters, and though it is a nice pink — almost as good as the classic 'Wildwood' — one *can* have enough of it.

Small gardens create intimate retreats within the expanse stretching to the riverbanks once intensively cultivated for rice production.

We have enjoyed and been successful with camellias in all their shades. Among the whites, 'Purity' has such superb flowers that it is worth growing even though it is a shy bloomer. 'Mrs. Hooper Cornell' is a thoroughly satisfactory white. Of the medium pinks, 'Oh Boy' and 'Melissa Duggan' are exceptionally good. Several good strong reds seem to have nautical associations: 'Admiral Nimitz', 'Pearl Harbor', and 'Pirate's Pride'. 'Magnoliaflora' is one of the most beautiful pale pinks, semi-double with a dozen or more petals in each blossom. 'Lady Vansittart' is a remarkable variegated camellia with great diversity of markings on its white background, which may be spattered or striped with pink. There are sports of this variety in pink or rose with darker markings.

I know I couldn't produce this kind of a garden today. Even if the labor were available it would be exorbitantly expensive. (I remember when we first came, our neighbors complained that we were spoiling the help by paying them a dollar a day.)

One recent planting maintains the old traditions. About 1820, one of the younger Heyward sons put in the allée of live oaks that still leads from the gate to the house. Ten years ago I put more of these trees out by the back entrance and they are already so well grown that I can see that in twenty or thirty years they will be marvelous specimens to delight future generations.

The live oaks lining the drive were planted in 1820.

Maxine Hull

DOGWOODS, HOUSTON, TEXAS

F OR MORE THAN fifty years, the gardens of Dogwoods have been planted and cared for so that they will glow with color in early March. And since 1936, they have been a feature of the annual Azalea Trail organized by the River Oaks Garden Club. In recent years this garden tour has brought eight to ten thousand people a weekend through the grounds to enjoy the tulips, dogwoods, camellias, and flowering peach trees as well as the azaleas that make Houston's early spring so spectacular. The three families that have owned Dogwoods have made a tradition of sharing with the community the special character of these seven acres with their live-oak-shaded lawns, their formalized plantings, and the cascades and pools of the lower bayou garden.

The house, designed by Birdsall Briscoe, a highly respected Houston architect, was built in 1927 for the Proctor family. It is next door to Bayou Bend, the mansion designed for Miss Ima Hogg by Briscoe's partner John Staub. Bayou Bend is now a museum and the River Oaks Garden Club helps to maintain its lovely grounds, which are also on the Azalea Trail every spring.

The property became "Dogwoods" after Mike Hogg, Miss Ima's brother, bought it from the Proctors, and it is *not* named for the trees. The story goes that the humorist Irvin S. Cobb, a friend of Mike's, saw the many dogs running loose and quipped, "You can't see the woods for the . . . dogs." Hence the name. And under the ledge that overlooks the pool in the lower garden, there are the heads of two dogs carved in the rock.

The gardens at Dogwoods were originally designed by C. C. Pat Fleming. Mr. Fleming is now retired, but for many years he was Houston's most revered landscape architect. My parents, Ethel and Ralph Thomas McDermott, bought Dogwoods about thirty years ago from Mike Hogg's widow. Then ten years ago, after my father's death, Mother moved to an apartment and we took over the estate. Through the years many of the oldest and largest azaleas and camellias had died or become very spindly and leggy. Much drastic pruning was required and we added many new plants. Gregory Catlow, a Houston landscape architect, helped to solve many of the problems confronting us. For the first four years a young horticulturist from the Northwest, Will Carlson, was our head gardener. I give him much credit for bringing the gardens back to their original beauty. He

developed a schedule for feeding, watering, spraying, pruning, and other maintenance that has made it possible for us to maintain the seven acres with only
three gardeners and the occasional help of Mr. Catlow.

We have six varieties of azaleas. They do well in Houston but require lots of
tender loving care. It is very difficult, nigh impossible, to determine exactly when
they will be at the height of their glory each spring. Every year we pray that their
blooming will coincide with the Azalea Trail.

In front of the house and around the swimming pool wing there are clipped
boxwood hedges that surround seasonal bedding plants; pink Aristocrat tulips in
spring, geraniums in summer, and begonias in autumn. The begonias bloom until
a freeze. Many Houston winters don't have a hard freeze. At first we planted the
tulips in the ground, but since they often bloomed too early or too late for the
Azalea Trail, we began potting them in the greenhouse so we could have some

*An early March mix of pink 'Aristocrat'
tulips, gerbera daisies, and white azaleas
fill the geometric beds that circle an old
crepe myrtle tree in the front garden.*

control over the flowering. It is quite a task to plant hundreds of tulips from pots to beds just a few days before the Trail each year, but it is certainly worth the effort to ensure that the visitors will have as pretty a sight as possible.

The many large crepe myrtle trees in the pool garden are an asset year round. They bloom in midsummer when little else thrives in our hot humid weather, but the contours of their gray trunks are pleasing in all seasons. In Houston they are often grown as trees by high pruning rather than in the usual way as bushes.

At the back of the house, looking out from the library and garden rooms, one can see the Clock Garden, so called because of the clock set in the brick wall at its far end. Double white 'Mrs. Gerbing' azaleas outline the perimeter of this garden and the central bricked beds are planted with a salmon 'Glen Dale' hybrid called Fashion. For the Trail the white bushes are bordered with blue ageratum, and white begonias edge the salmon azaleas. An arbor of yellow flowering cassia, not commonly seen in gardens here, covers a trellis below which stepping stones lead down to the lower garden.

The lower garden is lush with the intricate outlines and rich green tones of Southern Shield fern, Holly fern, American maidenhair, aralias and aspidistras.

White azaleas, 'Mrs. G.G. Gerbing', and salmon, reblooming 'Glen Dale' hybrids, 'Fashion', in the Clock Garden.

ESTATE GARDENS

From large boulders at the far end of the garden a waterfall cascades into a pool that empties into the ravine running through this area, flowing under a wooden foot bridge and on down to Buffalo Bayou. Azaleas are in abundance here, as are many varieties of *Camellia japonica*. Some of the best are 'Magnolia Flora', 'Purple Dawn', 'Debutante', 'Governor Mouton', 'Pink Perfection', and 'Empress'. There are many dogwoods, both pink and white. The ferns and ground covers have to be cut back in the spring if there has been a freeze, but by midsummer they are lushly abundant again. Summer also brings pink hydrangeas that thrive on the moist soil near the ravine and the tall fragrant white butterfly ginger (*Hedychium coronarium*), which blooms until late fall. On the far side of the ravine, a path meanders along an area shaded by *Magnolia grandiflora* underplanted with holly fern. Here too is a *Cryptomeria japonica,* an unusual tree for Houston.

On a trip to Japan I was very surprised to see gardens everywhere that resembled our lower garden and I have since wondered if its design was influenced by such Japanese gardens. Until our trip to the Orient I had only thought of Japanese gardens as the very stylized kind, with rocks and raked sand.

With its tall pines, oaks, and magnolias the lower garden is a favorite spot in summer. It is just gorgeous then, dark and damp, very much like a rain forest. It is so still, with only the sounds of birds and squirrels, that it is hard to believe we are only ten minutes from downtown Houston.

THE GARDEN OF

Eulalie Wagner

LAKEWOLD, TACOMA, WASHINGTON

LAKEWOLD is one of the oldest homes in Tacoma, built by the H. H. Alexanders, who created an extensive garden here at the turn of the century when Mr. Alexander was president of the Alaska-Pacific Steamship Company, which operated between Puget Sound and San Francisco.

A landmark from those early days is a stone and wooden fence extending the length of the property on Gravelly Lake Drive. Along this fence, the original shrubs of *Viburnum tomentosum* still display their array of white blossoms in the springtime, followed by berries in the summer and brilliant reddish foliage in the autumn. The old carriage house near the service entrance is now a greenhouse and potting shed; the name "Kitty" on one of the doors recalls the horse who once occupied a stall where plants now repose.

The most important architectural feature of the garden from those days is the long brick walk leading from the main house to a vine-covered tea house at the far end of the garden. In June, the old-fashioned musk rose 'Kathleen' forms a soft white bower over the entire latticework dome.

The garden is endowed with a very old stand of virgin Douglas fir, a native, as are the marvelous Gerry oaks that form a panorama along the water. So you see that Lakewold was aptly named by my husband's family, who came here in the early twenties, for it remains a veritable little forest on the lake shore.

As well as the majestic company of giant trees we have Mount Rainier, or at least a view of it. Its snow-capped peak is visible on clear sunny days from the quatrefoil-shaped pool, which lies on an axis with the mountain. Also in line with Mount Rainier is an antique lion fountain from England, my favorite garden piece, which spouts water from its mouth. If you want to know the hour, near by is a Queen Anne sundial.

When we first came to Lakewold in the spring of 1938, I was very much in awe of the place and felt I could never do it justice. I must say that our garden did live through some trying periods, particularly during World War II when we were short of help. My husband and son took turns cutting the lawn while I tended the boxwood parterres, transformed into a victory garden. Luckily we were able to engage an elderly farmer and his wife, who also cared for the cow we acquired and sheltered in Kitty's box stall.

*The shade garden under the "wolf tree," a Douglas fir unsuitable for lumbering, includes a maple (*Acer palmatum auratum*), Rhododendron bureavii, *and ground covers like variegated bishopweed (*Aegopodium podogaria variegatum*) and* Corydalis aurea.

White tulips and cherry blossoms frame the quatrefoil swimming pool.

ESTATE GARDENS   89

Topiary birds afloat on waves of blue crocus in the quatrefoil parterre beds.

In the 1950s I was rescued from my garden problems when I asked Thomas D. Church of San Francisco to come north and help me. His first, and very unexpected, venture was to create a shade garden. As we strolled down the brick walk during his introductory visit he noticed an unusually shaped fir tree, some two hundred years old. Called a "wolf" tree, it was scorned by our Northwest lumbermen. I told Mr. Church that the area of the tree was my bête noir as nothing but deadly weeds would grow under its shade. His immediate reaction was to feature this exotic-looking tree by forming a pebbled path around its trunk and placing a very old Buddha figure as a focal point. At the feet of the Buddha, which was found in Japan by my husband's uncle, Major Briggs, is a small pool. Here I have dug in many of my early-blooming plants where they can be admired from the glass-enclosed garden room on drizzly spring mornings when the first rhododendron blooms appear. No one need wander far from the house to view cyclamen, slipper orchids, bloodroot, and trillium. Also vying for attention here are hellebores, dogtooth violets, ground covers such as gaultheria, vancouveria, and bunchberry (*Cornus canadensis*), and a collection of ferns. The leatherleaf fern (*Polypodium scouleri*) nestles in the bare upper branches of the wolf tree as it does in the Olympic Mountains.

One of the boxwood-edged parterre beds along one side of the brick walk repeats the motif of the quatrefoil, a design also incorporated in the paving of the tea house floor. The flowers in these parterre beds change with the seasons but the center of attention remains the topiary peacock and attendant swans. A sea of blue crocus fills the beds in the spring so that from a distance the birds appear to be gliding on water.

When we first came to Lakewold we enjoyed a marvelous view of Gravelly Lake but gradually this was marred by houses on the opposite shore. Then meandering through an uncultivated area down by the lake I discovered a pristine view. I considered creating a rock garden at the end of the path, but when I told my plan to Mr. Church he promptly dismissed it. He warned me that all the gardeners (myself included) would spend most of their time in the rockery while my beautiful formal garden turned into a shambles. Nonetheless I went ahead. Needless to say the rockery is a nice contrast to the formal garden and one of the paths leading to it, through rare rhododendrons, still offers the best view of the lake. This is my "Northwest Garden," originally planted with natives. The rocks as well as the plants were carefully selected and brought down from the Olympics to be carefully arranged true to nature. Waterfalls splash over the rocks to a pool at the foot of the hillside. Later I couldn't resist adding species from other countries and now hardy orchids, various forms of *Cypripedium,* and *Pleione* bloom there.

Not many of my friends ever visited the rockery, so once again Mr. Church came to my rescue and made it more inviting by creating a lookout from which to view the whole incline with its waterfalls and pools and, finally, the lake itself.

To the left, from the same vantage point, one has a glimpse of the grotto created after a visit to Queluz, a country palace near Lisbon. That lovely garden with its grotto designed by the Frenchman J. B. Robillon inspired my version, where the water drips through clumps of native and hybrid ferns.

On the lower hillside is a comparatively dry scree area. Here I specialized in various forms, deciduous and evergreen, of *Lewisia*, including *L. Tweedyi*, the largest in the group, *L. columbiana*, *L. nevadensis*, *L. cotyledon*, and *L. rediviva*. They are exceptionally difficult to grow in our dampness, as their habitat is exposed, gravelly and rocky slopes or rock crevices. The *Lewisia*, all native to the Western states, were named after Meriwether Lewis of the Lewis and Clark Expedition, while Frank Tweedy, one of the surveyors who routed the Northern Pacific Railroad, first sighted the species *L. tweedyi*.

One of my favorite parts of this garden is a little knoll called the "Gray Scree." It started out as a "Rosaceae Garden," as our garden club was studying this family. Among the species were a few gray plants which looked so stunning against the gray rocks that I was tempted to eliminate all others and have a gray garden, although I did leave a background planting of *Dryas octopetala*, dating to the Rosaceae Period. It qualified, I felt, as its seed pods (silk seed heads) form gray poof balls that cling until blown away with the wind. Many of the gray plants are troublesome, not tolerating the rainy season, but their silvery foliage is worth the effort.

From here a swimmer can see Mount Rainier on a clear day.

*Four unusual rhododendrons by the
second waterfall:* R. lepidostylum, R.
recurvoides, R. forestii repens, *and*
R. yakusimanum; *with* Acer
palmatum dissectum, *weeping
Canadian hemlock, and* Linnaea
borealis *in the background.*

I am one of those uncontrollable collectors. During the past forty years, I
have moved through phases, my first being rhododendrons, which I've never really
given up. Next came my roses. I am always adding a few of the new hybrids as
well as some of the very old ones, such as 'Madame Plantier' and 'Sombrier', and
a new "old" shrub, 'Mermaid'. Then I began acquiring maple trees, and cherries,
and on and on. Finally, I took up my latest interest, the alpine plants in my rockery,
an absorbing hobby to which there is no end.

While I worked over my collections, my husband gathered a collection of
exotic trees. He obtained seeds and seedling trees when we traveled around the
world in 1953, visiting arboreta and private forests. Upon our return a conifer
garden was started on a hillock commanding a singular view of Gravelly Lake
silhouetted through his trees. Today, this area is becoming a veritable "second"
forest and an uncommon collection. A few deciduous trees have been added, such
as the dove tree, *Davidia involucrata,* also called the handkerchief tree; *Acer griseum*
(paper bark maple), a tree with excoriating bark; and *Acer palmatum* 'Shishigashira'
(lion's head), compact and stubby — ideal for small landscapes. My husband's
collection includes *Sequoia sempervirens* as well as *Sequoiadendron giganteum.* One
tree, the dawn redwood, standing alone in the middle of a bed of grass that is
fertilized at least four times a year, may be one of the biggest in the Northwest.

Mr. Church's annual visits, along with his books, were a continuous education
for me. I have tried to follow his four requisites: Function, Continuity, Scale, and
Simplicity. The drive, parking area, and paths must function well for all occasions.
For continuity one section must flow into another with a visual transition beyond.
The large expanses of lawn are appropriate to the scale of our gigantic indigenous
trees. Above all I seek simplicity, which I feel has been achieved as the garden has
acquired an aura of tranquility.

The plantings around the waterfall in the rock garden include a golden Japanese maple in the center background, the Rhododendron tsangpoenses prunifolium *(left), the lavender* Rhododendron arboreum, *the red-leaved* Acer palmaturm desojo *and the low red-flowering* Rhododendron forestii repens *on the bank. Marsh marigold (*Caltha palustris*) and deerfern (*Blechnum spicant*) appear in the lower left corner.*

THE GARDEN OF

Carol Ann Mackay

EXCELSIOR, MINNESOTA

Lythrum and milkweed at the lakeside.

S LONG AS I can remember I've been in love with Christmas Lake and the peninsula there that we now call home. As a teenager I used to marvel at the lake, so clear that we could see fish scatter in water thirty feet deep as we skied over them. To test if we could live here year-round, Harvey and I rented a tiny cabin for the summer after our marriage. I would paddle down to the end of the point at 5:30 A.M. to cast for bass. Once in a while I'd share the sunrise with a pair of mink who lived for years at the base of an old willow that will survive us all.

The clear, potable lake water is still our only drinking water source and the water supply for everything that grows here. We live surrounded by masses of white water lilies and a seemingly endless pink horizon of lythrum in summer. In autumn there are the blazing oranges, reds, and rusts of sugar maples, oaks, and sumac, in winter the glowing color of red-stemmed dogwood against white snow, and in spring the fluorescent yellow-greens of new leaves.

I have always looked at our land as a work-in-progress, much as I consider a painting, drawing, or sculpture as I work on it over a period of time. My career as a serious gardener began one late April morning about a dozen years ago when I scattered half a pound of seeds of shasta daisy 'Alaska' and half a pound of coreopsis seeds into a tilled bed the length of a football field that meandered along the lythrum and cattail swamp that borders the lake. My initial idea was to paint a fat ribbon of yellow and white against the lush lavender-pink lythrum that bloomed without fail each July. That summer I battled crabgrass and drought. The second summer I had my colorful blast of daisies and coreopsis all right, but it came weeks before the lythrum bloomed and after that I had nothing!

I had a lot to learn about dense clay soil that sticks in globs to our boots until mid-May . . . about our formidable climate with its late-April snowfalls and mid-September freezes . . . the gorgeous but dry, hot summers, the preposterously cold winters, and the ridiculously short growing season. But having been born with that stubbornness we in the Midwest are known for, I have, over the years, devised a formula for a great garden in a cold climate. Plant the best, the brightest, and the most of your favorite flowers. Overlap them for constant bloom. Love them while they flower, share them with your friends, and don't cry when they freeze solid at the end of September. Then move indoors and grow orchids on

your windowsill, or if you're fortunate enough to have a greenhouse, dig up a storm in there.

First I made a list of absolutely foolproof, climate-proof bulbs and perennials. I chose all my favorite bright colors, including some that would relate the garden to the lythrum swamp beyond. I was interested in great masses of bright color, the brighter the better. We have enough months of that sea of white! Now after years of trial and error, lots of reading, much consultation with my gardening friends, the University of Minnesota Arboretum staff, lily growers, and professional perennial growers who have the land under their fingernails and the climate in their bones, the following scenario has evolved.

The first harbingers of spring are seven *Magnolia stellata* that have survived eight years of Minnesota harassment. They bloom bravely in mid-April, a perfect reminder to begin spring cleanup. About the same time a solitary apricot tree blooms profusely, but in vain. Its companion was killed by hungry rabbits and it will be several years before its new pals will pollinate it. With the glow of new leaves come the tulips, a mid-May riot of Darwins in yellows, reds, oranges,

The flower garden stretches for a hundred yards along the lythrum and cattail swamp that borders Christmas Lake.

salmons, and every variation in between. We've planted them by the thousands throughout the perennial border and in large beds at our front door.

While we wait for the first perennials we are happily occupied with a purple and white lilac hedge that seven years after its planting is finally rewarding us with splendid bouquets and fragrance. This spring I will learn if two new beds of deciduous Exbury and Mollis azaleas have survived the cold. Apple trees, crabs, hawthorns, and shadblow help usher in a Minnesota spring.

As the tulips pale and the iris and lilies push upward, from mid-May to June first I begin setting out cleome, snapdragons, marigolds, petunias, zinnia, and blue salvia, with the help of Theresa and Cindy, who are babysitters turned gardener's helpers. We hoe in a generous supply of 5-10-5 fertilizer and, with the annuals in place, mulch the entire bed in three inches of cocoa bean hulls and hope never to weed again.

Sometime in June, we expect the first splendid clumps of bearded iris. They are accompanied by a parade of Siberian iris and a thick back hedge of *Iris pseudacorus* that sends up handsome beardless bright yellow flowers similar in form to the Siberian. Later the five-foot-tall spikes of their dark green leaves form another barrier against the ever-encroaching lythrum. In yet another attempt to establish a buffer zone, the iris is backed by a hedge of red-stemmed dogwood.

Each year I wait impatiently for wonderful stands of Asiatic lilies that arrive along with the veterans of my first efforts, the shastas and the coreopsis. There are bright red-orange Maltese cross about this time too, providing a piercing accent. If by now you suspect that this is a garden of warm colors, you are correct. The annual blue salvia provides the only strong cool color through the summer.

Next come huge clumps of old-fashioned lemon lily (*Hemerocallis lilioaspho-*

Gloriosa daisies, phlox, petunias, marigolds, and daylilies, with the fading flowers of Macleaya cordata *at the back of the border. A baby-sitter turned gardener's helper is busy with midsummer cleanup.*

delus) and a wide variety of newer daylily hybrids. These now extend far beyond the original perennial bed, and swatches of daylilies in red, oranges, yellows, and pinks now meander along most of our lakeshore. They intertwine with long ribbons of Royal Standard hosta that also borders the lilacs along the driveway; the flowering shrubs and hosta act as a transition between the grass and the woods. In August when the hosta blooms the fragrance floats on the breeze and the whole peninsula lights up with its white flowers. In fall, the bright color of its turning leaves paints a strand of yellow along the still-green grass.

By July most of the annuals are in full bloom in a dazzling explosion of color along with masses of phlox, perennial sunflower (*Heliopsis* 'Summer Sun') and the much mentioned lythrum. Our sudden summer heat, which is as extreme as our winter cold, does wonders for heat-loving annuals, which bloom in great profusion and tide us over from the last lilies and daylilies to the first chrysanthemum bursts in early September. However, the same heat will delay the mums from setting buds on time and often even early varieties will bloom two or three weeks late.

Gardens in Minnesota always come to a violent end. After that first unpredictable early killing frost, only the cushion mums go on blooming under the onslaught of slush and early snow. But when the worst happens and the first night temperature of 25°F is finally assured, I postpone the decimation one time by lugging canvases, blankets, and plastic tarps down to the garden, usually around midnight. Working by the headlights of my van, I cover what I can and chop down what I can't and haul armfuls of flowers to the truck. The next morning when I've regained my sanity, I arrange gigantic bouquets of mums all around the house and give them away to friends.

I'm very fortunate to have a greenhouse, but it was Harvey's idea as much as mine. In a valiant effort to grow luxuriant foliage plants in our old house I finally installed ceilings full of growlights in the bathrooms. My husband got tired of wending his way to the shower through attacking Sprengeri ferns and skin-slicing yuccas. To his dismay, however, I have recently discovered that our present bathroom, which faces south and east and is less humid than the greenhouse, is perfect for tomatoes (Vendor or Ontario Hybrid red), African violets, and Rieger begonias. It is also the best place to winter-over our geranium trees and plants. Once ensconced around the bathtub they bloom nonstop from January to April, when I cut them back before moving them outside in late May.

The cool greenhouse (50–55°F at night) often gets as high as 80° plus in our bright winter sun. This temperature range is fine for cymbidium orchids, azaleas, camellias, and an assortment of foliage plants. After some experimenting, however, and the realization that plants are among the earth's most adaptable organisms, the current assortment in my greenhouse includes night-blooming jasmine, lemon, grapefruit, and tangerine trees (slightly bonsaied but fruit bearing), gerberas, cattleya, phalaenopsis, oncidium and dendrobium orchids, bougainvillea that cascades showers of pink and red from January to June, and parsley, mint, scallions, and Bibb lettuce for winter consumption. Even castoff greens from greenhouse and kitchen have their use. They feed a clan of rabbits that used to girdle annually every shrub or young tree tender enough to chew on. Now come December, or

Ribbons of red cushion mums and yellowing hosta leaves echo the bands of autumn color in the maples above.

*Red-stemmed dogwood adds subtle color
to the winter landscape while forming a
barricade against the aggressive
lythrum.*

whenever the ground is completely snow covered, they appear daily for breakfast and dinner near the greenhouse door and the bushes thrive.

Meanwhile, outside the self-designed conservatory we call home, there is color of a more subtle sort. Red-stemmed dogwoods glisten against the snow, rusty oak leaves cling to the charcoal brown-black of branches. Leafless branches of weeping willows glow yellow-orange, and birches and aspens add subtle monochromes. Cardinals, jays, chickadees, and sparrows are grateful for the frozen berries adorning the mountain ashes, highbush cranberries, nannyberry and chokecherry bushes.

Midwinter is a time to pause . . . time to putter in the greenhouse after dinner, to work on plant sketches that are currently the raw material for a new series of sculpture, to build a fire and pore over a stack of catalogues. We wait quietly, storing up energy to begin anew.

Georgianna Orsini

PAWLING, NEW YORK

I SUPPOSE I've always longed for something more than what I am or have. And like any other appetite, hunger has made me greedy. Had I the means I would join those fabled shoppers of Beverly Hills buying my baubles by the dozen, in every shape and color, eager for those fleeting satisfactions.

On the other hand I have a vigilant Puritan conscience which insists on my usefulness and that my pleasures must be earned. As a gardener I am able to indulge, if not resolve, both aspects of my character. There isn't a species, color, or scheme I haven't considered and usually tried. I've had seasons and reasons for planting petunias, begonias, peonies, chrysanthemums and roses. Heady with imperial powers, I act on my likes and dislikes, fiercely eliminating plants that don't meet my expectations, but allowing some of them to infiltrate their way back into my good graces. Petunias were banished for a season or two; I got tired of their soppiness along my borders after it rained, but the substitute ageratums, for all their coveted blue, don't look full until August, and so a few straggler petunias have started to polka-dot the edges again. Peonies were once awarded a great prominence befitting their opulent plumes and drowning perfume, until I had to reckon that their display lasted about as long as an old-fashioned ball. So they have been relegated to a less conspicuous position, which I regret during the one week they flourish. Last year I started four kinds of chrysanthemum listed in the Park Seed catalogue, excited by their late blooming period. But only last-minute charity permitted them to bloom, as it was disappointing to see them without the accompaniment of other flowers and all their neighbors already rested on the compost heap.

Perhaps there is no flower that is truly dependable, or worse, if there is, it is a bore. That's the careless attitude I have toward yarrows, feverfew, evening primrose, artemisia and the early Shasta daisy, for all of which I was once grateful. But it's not a very long list. On the other hand there's very little I haven't done to have roses, none of which want to stay more than a season or two, and one year there was a disheartening 80 percent disaster after our polar siege of a winter. But their raving beauty and satisfying blooms make me slavish. Through much trial and no help from commercial growers who raise them all in milder areas, making me wish I was the subzero test garden, I now put up chicken-wire baskets

The "Swan Lake Garden" planted in the soft shadings of faded romance. Four lavender tree roses en pointe punctuate the ageratum, petunias, and dusty miller.

Tall lilies, delphinium, and snakeroot alongside a rustic trellis. Soft gray drifts of artemisia and clumps of red beebalm among the pinks of phlox, snapdragons, and daylilies.

Yellows are banished from the gardens
near the house to the area near the pool.
Rudbeckias, heleniums, and giant
zinnias light the path.

around each rose and fill these cages up with leaves that act as a better insulator than the recommended dirt, which traps the damp. At the last I bring in snow fencing to surround the larger beds as a stockade against the desiccating winds and I tell myself I now pull through most of those that once would have been lost.

Another favorite, delphiniums, are less sensitive to the cold and grow easily from seed. As insurance, I start a new batch every fall, and that way I have a reserve to plug up any holes in the main garden with a skyscraper blue that makes any nearby yellow or pink glow with added intensity. I've also conceded what Puritan remnants I had of a vegetable garden, giving up those practicalities for a nursery garden and just such things like extra delphiniums, which I find more essential than the zucchini I never did pick until it was the size of a caveman's club.

If I am ever reduced to one flower through fatigue, experience, or long-felt gratitude, it will not be hard to choose the tuberous begonia. Even limited to one tiny terrace, their gay blossoms are lavish and continuous enough to suggest a garden. I start them in February, and by June they are in their 8- to 9-inch pots on a three-tiered stand. At eye level they are easy to tend without doing deep knee bends and they provide a blaze of warm yellows, oranges, and reds. No whites, as they are too inhibiting.

I save the whites for my more ethereal Swan Lake Garden, which is plotted in terms of the sweet sad shadings of romance: silver artemisia, blue and white delphiniums, phlox, and iris surround a baroque fountain, lifted by four lavender tree roses en pointe.

Such decisions were preceded by a long uncertainty, which began to erode during my three years in Italy, on a Tuscan farm. There life is not made a burden,

but an excuse for pleasure wherever, and whenever, possible. Before I went there my gardening was limited to a small bed of zinnias and a longer shelf full of books, ambitiously read. My knowledge apparently increased, but my garden stayed as it was. All of this had nothing to do with the natural, even atavistic ease with which my Italian friends instructed me. It was all simple, not the result of consulting books, nor of using formulas or expensive sprays; it was a matter of employing good sense. And water, either early in the morning or at dusk. For earth they pointed to the forest floor, or the particularly prized compost from the chestnut tree or broom. Their flowers were proof, looking as lush and well cared for as any member of their families. Dina's spread of purple and red anemones and rainbow ranunculus were for me an inspiring new addition to spring. Our farmer's wife, Lucia, was equally proud of her balloon-sized hydrangeas growing out of discarded tins, receiving the same diligent attention as her fattest pig.

I was less inspired by the pinched and shaped contortions exhibited in more suburban gardens in Italy, the mercilessly pruned pyracantha and other topiary, but the ordinary need for beauty touched me deeply and I found myself in easy conversation with anyone with a plant. That way I gathered a whole hedgeful of purple morning glory from a vine crowning a nearby village well. Some of it crossed the seas with me home. I also massed the wild blue iris down a mile of old stone wall, much the way I later worked here with our native tiger lily in a massive planting that blooms predictably loud and high every Fourth of July. I still have the Florentine blue iris by the pool, and it is the only iris not subject to the borer that rots its more refined purchased hybrid progeny. But of course nothing will ever grow for me here the way the roses climbed my olive trees, showering the branches with pink and yellow blooms, and a few less olives. And to think that once I had a field full of sunflowers from a few handfuls of seed.

But the other happiness has been my transplantable experience. I am so easily excited and enchanted by seeing a garden, and with each success more than willing to work toward another. What does it all really require? Not a lot really, but a constancy I never suspected I was capable of. From spring to fall I don't bother with the exhausting excitements of New York City, but preserve a simpler state of mind and the quietness needed to recognize when a bit of watering or clipping is required, if only for ten minutes. Besides which my fingernails are indelibly dirty. Isak Dinesen's distrust of any woman who hadn't experienced an orgy or childbirth might well have been extended to one who hadn't gardened. Sometimes I just lie down on my bed, too much of an earthworm to bother with anything as civilized as a bath.

Twice a week for five hours I have help in the garden. Andy Pollack works nights in the state mental hospital and knows how to care for living things; patients and plants respond to his innate sensitivity. He judges the weeds not by their names but by their vigor and he is the one I trust with the cultivation that is the only way I know of keeping ahead of them. He is also expert at edging the long lines that make picture frames for each bed. He has also never complained at trying to find one more hole in the rock-infested soil, although the spots all seem more tractable to a stick of dynamite than a mere pick and shovel.

My husband, were he not otherwise employed as a businessman, would make an excellent gardener. He says he is not interested but is quite vociferous about appearances: with flowers as with women, no detail escapes his perfectionist eye. On hot summer days, knowing my flightiness with the hose, he will water everything, pointing out how much more saturated are the plants in his charge. Part of the reason the begonias command so much admiration is his scrupulous staking and dead-heading; also they are right next to his elbow as he waits for a late breakfast or dinner.

One can put a lot of effort into friends, into getting an education, playing the piano, writing a poem, cooking a meal — all of which I try to do — and into making a garden. There is an evanescence to it all; just as you manage a grasp, some further knowledge qualifies your hold. And though a garden's joys are transient, how many mornings I wake up prompted to go outside and look to see what has happened. How many evenings I see the garden under the flattering lights and it seems I had nothing to do with it. Although I remember and know I did, that becomes irrelevant, separating from me like a woodland bird's song. Intact, pristine, on a flight of its own, I am free of it — to marvel, part of a paradise I never thought was mine.

Like millefiori paperweights, the beds are crammed with a mix of annuals (snapdragons and cleome) and perennials (coreopsis, phlox, daylilies, beebalm, and Asiatic lilies) tempered with the grays of stachys, lavender, and artemisia.

THE GARDEN OF

Faith Mackaness

CORBETT, OREGON

ORTHWEST OREGON has the best bad climate in the world for gardeners. There are a sufficient number of cyclonic storms to keep us stimulated, but not enough bad weather to be permanently discouraging. Sixty to seventy inches of rain annually (and little air pollution) keep the local landscape luxurious. Summers are usually warm and dry, and winters milder than in other areas of the same latitude. We live twenty miles east of Portland, near the western entrance to the spectacular Columbia River gorge, weathermaker extraordinary. Its east winds prune the local Douglas firs so drastically that they resemble flags silhouetted against the sky. The foothills topography, the ubiquitous windbreaks, and the location of buildings determine what plants will grow where, in the wilds, on the adjacent farms, and in the gardens around Corbett.

We purchased our house, a small remodeled schoolhouse, in 1954, and once settled, Frank persuaded a fellow Briton, Desmond Muirhead, now a well-known recreation city planner, to draw up a landscape plan for our acre of garden. I had grown up in a gardening family on the Gulf Coast and had done graduate work in botany and ecology in the South. Although my knowledge of temperate-zone plants was minimal, I could count on my husband's expertise. He had trained at Cambridge University Botanic Garden, Kew, and elsewhere before serving as an agricultural and horticultural consultant. Soon I became totally immersed in the art, craft, and discipline of growing hardy plants.

By 1956 the space for the herbaceous perennial border that Frank and Desmond had decided I would create was laid out on the north side of the house facing the new lawn and backed by the requisite English yew hedge — then a thin row of lining-out stock. I had never met an English border, and Frank's gifts of books by William Robinson, Gertrude Jekyll, and Richard Sudell did not allay my fears nor end my confusion. Visits to gardens, study of nursery catalogues and much reference to *Hortus II* and the *Royal Horticultural Society Dictionary* led to my first mail order. The plants that arrived had apparently been in cold storage all winter but began to grow en route from Ohio, and when I planted the tangled mass of roots and shoots most of them rotted off in the Oregon "mist." I had better results that autumn with white and pink gas plants (*Dictamnus alba* and *D. a. Ruben*), the lovely daylily 'Hyperion', and giant mugwort (*Artemisia lactiflora*),

Yellow and white varieties of Verbascum chaixii.

Muscari carpet the woodland bulb garden beneath the moss- and lichen-covered limbs of thirty-year-old staghorn sumac.

The west end of the perennial border, with the bulb woodland beyond the yew hedge. *Sedum purpureum* '*Autumn Joy*', *lavender, and a* Sedum maximum atropurpureum *in the center front of the border with a mound of baptisia in fruit behind. Two filipendulas, the white queen of the meadow (*F. ulmaria*) and the pink queen of the prairie (*F. rubra venusta*) provide height in the back of the border together with spikes of* Cimicifuga racemosa *and a Joe Pye weed with buds that already soar above the hedge.*

the only artemesia that doesn't melt in our rains; they are still performing well. Low creeping phlox (*P. subulata*) took off like thunder at the front of the border and inspired me to use alpines and rock plants there. As I became more knowledgeable I gave the phlox to ranker beginners and sought choicer subjects, *Campanula carpatica*, and *Geranium cinereum* 'Ballerina', *Verbascum* 'Lelitia', and *Iris pallida variegata*.

Five years later when the border began to look "clothed," as Frank called it, he decided that it was time for everything to be lifted and divided. The divisions were held in the nursery while the border was redug and fertilized. After replanting, I saw to my horror that Frank had left large bare spaces between the clumps and even larger ones around each group of clumps, which I could visualize as stages for weeds. There was no room for any new plants and even worse there would be periods with no interest at all. Besides, there was a truckload of duplicates to be disposed of. I was devastated!

It was not until I visited England and Scotland and saw the extensive perennial borders of the large estates and botanic gardens there that I understood why traditional practices did not work for me in the Northwest. My eighty-five-by-eighteen-foot border doesn't have the space for masses of continuous bloom, and neither trained help nor many of the better European cultivars were available. But I didn't want to rely on the usual American method of gardening with annuals either. So I decided to find my own compromise, and went back to the gardening books again.

Alan Bloom's paperback manual, *Perennials for Troublefree Gardening,* with its novel method of rating the social behavior of perennials, became my gardening bible. One year I ordered only seeds and plants he rated 8 to 10. Frank gave me Graham Stuart Thomas's *Color in the Winter Garden.* This book influenced me even more than Thomas's later monumental *Perennial Garden Plants.* Kenneth A.

Beckett's *Growing Hardy Perennials* fills in basic information that Graham Thomas assumes that even neophytes know intuitively. Now I have a second edition of *Perennial Garden Plants* to replace my well-worn original, and I find the author and my husband easier to understand. Have I grown wiser as well as older?

Although seasoned European gardeners would think it sacrilege, I finally decided that plants requiring constant dividing, staking, and spraying did not justify the work and time involved. First to go were the tall delphiniums. A candelabra-like hybrid mullein, *Verbascum chaixii,* with rosy-centered yellow flowers, now takes their place. (Because it is short-lived, its seedlings must be spared in clean-ups.) Russell lupines were the next victims, and anyway, *Phlomis russeliana* is more exciting throughout the season. Late-blooming subjects like coneflowers, helenium, and Michaelmas daisies were allowed because they can be cut back half way early in July to encourage sturdy branching. I seldom remove spent flowering stalks, since they provide natural supports for undisciplined associates. Groups of globe thistles and sea hollies are placed to contain aggressive loosestrife and wandering Peruvian lilies. Dwarf shrubby lavenders in the front rows prevent

Plants for architectural interest are Acanthus spinosus *(left) and* Cimicifuga racemosa, *pictured with the broad bronzy leaves and buds of* Ligularia 'Desdemona' *(right).*

Hypericum 'Hidcote' is a handsome, reliable shrub that blooms most of the summer if dead flowers are removed. It can be cut to the ground every few years to rejuvenate it.

spiderwort hybrids (*Tradescantia* × *andersonii*) from flopping over the lawn. Late flowering cultivars of *Sedum telephium* and *S. spectabile* form dense clumps that are guaranteed to keep the taller bellflowers behind them upright. Hardy geraniums of the *G. sylvaticum* and *G. psilostemon* persuasion can shore up spiky background perennials that are drawn up by the shade of the hedge. Moreover, given half a chance hardy geraniums will cover any bare spot; I have used dozens of species and cultivars of this family to fill the border with their dancing flowers.

To keep densely planted perennials healthy they must be well fed. An annual covering of compost, with occasional applications of dolomite and 15-15-15 fertilizer have kept ours floriferous and their foliage luxuriant. Strong plants seem to resist most natural enemies, and worms, caterpillars, and spittlebugs can be removed manually if one has the stomach for it. There was a time when the spraying and dusting program for our hybrid tea roses and show dahlias controlled our lives. No more! Our chief concern these days is our voracious mollusk population. We have used hundreds of pounds of metaldehyde dust and pellets over the years in what always appeared to be a losing battle. Now Frank's small colony of Khaki Campbell ducks have joined the battle: he lets them out daily to cruise for slugs, snails, and cutworms; then they are herded back to the pool and duckhouse where they produce their delectable large eggs.

Since I can't achieve the successive masses of color of the large European borders in our small layout, I rely on architectural plants for effect. They are decorative in leaf, color, and fruit, and thus do not need cutting back after flowering. *Acanthus spinosus* and *Baptisia australis* are good examples.

The border is usually approached from the south and fortunately many of the daisylike flowers face that way. A bite is taken out of the center of the border, and it is only twelve feet wide there; I try to balance the halves by repeating similar colors and shapes on either side. Tough plants like Joe Pye weed (*Eupatorium purpureum*), oxeye daisies, sunflowers and the taller goldenrods fill the back rows because they can compete with the invasive roots of the yew. Decorative tall plants, like *Selenium tenuifolium* with its jade green dissected leaves, are sometimes used in the middle and front rows to break up the stairstep look. The Himalayan windflower, *Morina longifolia*, is a star all summer in the center front. In spring its thistly rosettes are flanked by *Euphorbia polychroma*, in summer its elongating flowering stems by clusters of brilliant blue *Gentiana uniflora*, and then, as its flowers change to equally decorative fruits, by masses of old rose coneflowers.

With the first killing frosts of October the spotlight turns to the bulbs that carpet a woodland, one-hundred-and-fifty feet by thirty feet, along our south boundary. The thirsty roots of six clumps of cutleaf weeping birch absorb any moisture that falls in spring and autumn and so provide the extensive period of dormancy required for bulbs of Mediterranean origin. Beyond are three forms of sumac which flaunt a fiery red after the birch leaves fall. As nights get colder the carpet below erupts with myriads of pink and white hardy cyclamen and a long succession of colchicum. Over the years I have tried most of the treasures pictured in Patrick M. Synge's *Collins Guide to Bulbs* as well as more recent discoveries of plant hunters.

The plumes of Aruncus diocus, *or goat's beard, wave above clumps of* thalictrum, phlox, beebalm, *and* echinops.

The woodland has been extended to grow anemones, hepaticas, and pulsatillas; I have dreamed of these ever since seeing them in Scandinavia in 1971, massed in the woodlands around Oslo. My plants, grown from seed, are beginning to multiply successfully. Some of the trees and shrubs are very special: a weeping golden ash, a fothergilla and a disanthus give spectacular fall raiment, and witch hazel and winter sweet add spring fragrance. On February 1, 1983, I picked over one hundred flowering specimens from overhead and underfoot to show a local garden club that there *is* color in the winter garden.

Having achieved three score and ten, Frank and I plan to move eventually to a small ground-floor apartment in a retirement village with enough garden space for a bulb bed, cold frames, troughs, and perhaps an alpine house. Frank will want to keep his hand in the community vegetable plot. When my own infirmities curtail more strenuous activities, I hope to disinter my microscopes and return to the enchanting world of bryophytes. But thirty years of shared enthusiasm with a professionally trained gardening husband and the contributions of plant loving friends have created an environment that will be difficult to leave and impossible to forget.

THE GARDEN OF

Jane Kerr Platt

PORTLAND, OREGON

AVING BEEN BORN and brought up on the outskirts of Portland where my Scottish father was creating a magnificent garden, Elk Rock, it is small wonder that I developed at an early age a love of gardening. In 1939, I married and moved to the small house my husband owned, situated on two and a half acres of land high in the West Hills above Portland. John has always claimed I married him for his property. Indeed, I might well have, what with the eighteen inches or more of friable acid loam soil that covered what was once an old orchard.

The land is a rectangle with good drainage, sloping toward the north and west. The entire property is surrounded by hedges, half of old cedar, the rest of holly. They give not only privacy but protection from the winds. Four old apple trees remaining from the orchard are used as the focal points for the house and garden. The acre and a half of sweeping lawn is surrounded by beds of varying depths containing many rare trees, shrubs, plants, and bulbs. Magnolias, maples, stewartias, and davidias are of special interest.

We began the garden after completing a new house in 1941, but progress was slowed by World War II and John's absence in the navy. Then a new start had to be made after a disastrous early November freeze in 1955. For three years from 1959, with more experience and more time as my children were growing up, I worked with a talented young landscape designer to give the garden the form it has today. Many of the trees and shrubs planted during this period were very small specimens, so the garden did not begin to mature for some time.

Our garden is composed of smaller gardens within a larger plan. Each has its own character and purpose, but I like to think of each as being an intrinsic part of the whole, which because of the abundance of light we planned for maximum autumn color.

The first area to be developed was the Gravel Garden, in the southeast corner, the highest point of the property. Planned as a source of relief from the sometimes overwhelming green of the lawn, it is rectangular, with narrow wooden edges paralleling the boundary lines. Two diagonal strips, eighteen inches wide and made of pea gravel, divide this rectangle into three large panels of contrasting rock and gravel, giving a textured effect to the whole area. Varied and unusual trees and shrubs grow on the east side above a low rock wall, over which cascade dwarf

Crocosmia masoniorum *in the west border.*

Looking up the slope of the rock garden through the spires of Picea glauca albertiana conica *toward a dwarf cedar of Lebanon* (Cedrus libani nana) *and two* Juniperus virginiana *'Skyrocket'.*

trees and smaller shrubs. From this area, broad steps descend between an old *Acer griseum* and a *Magnolia* × *loebneri* 'Spring Snow' to a wide grass path leading to the Rock Garden.

The Rock Garden, started in 1978, was our most recent development. For some time we had our eye on some magnificent layered basalt in an abandoned quarry on the slopes of Mount Hood. The moving of these rocks, many of which weighed two to three tons, to our place required ingenuity as well as a certain degree of "derring-do." Both were supplied by my husband with the assistance of a U-Rent mobile crane and a large flatbed truck. The placing of these rocks was an arduous but exciting episode, and they serve as a constant reminder that nothing is impossible if there is a will to do it.

This Rock Garden is a great joy to me. I find there is a progression in gardening interests, from the first enthusiasm for planting of trees and shrubs to — eventually — the fascination with the gemlike plants of the alpine world. Also this Rock Garden finally gave me a suitable home for the dwarf conifers I had collected over forty years. A small book could be written on its contents, but a

A bay of perennial flowers in the west border of flowering trees and shrubs. Left to right: Alstromeria ligtu *hybrids,* Eremurus bungei, Allium giganteum, Papaver somniferum, *and* Crocosmia masoniorum *in the foreground.*

Fall color in the gravel garden: from left to right, Euonymous alatus compacta, *two* Acer dissectum, *a golden* Corylopsis pauciflora, *a copper* Rhododendron schlippenbachia *and* Euonymus alatus. *The evergreen on the left is a dwarf* Sequoiadendron sempervirens, *and the large conifer on the right is the native cedar,* Thuya plicata *'Hogan's Variety'.*

few favorites stand out: a double white trillium (*T. grandiflorum album plenum*), a double deep pink hepatica (*H. acutiloba*), lady's slipper (*Calceolaria darwinii*), summer- and autumn-flowering gentians, many saxifrages, and a variety of dwarf iris — a specialty.

A long undulating bed extends from the Gravel Garden down to the southwest corner of our property. Here, magnolias, stewartias, and conifers culminate with a huge and unique weeping form of *Sequoiadendron giganteum pendulum,* a redwood relative. Close by is a *Chamaecyparis nootkatensis,* with drooping branchlets, brought back as a tiny seedling from the base of Mt. St. Helens years before its catastrophic eruption. One of the most striking trees in this area is *Prunus serrula,* a cherry whose ribbons of red peeling bark glow in the setting winter sun.

Another long irregular bed extends the length of our west boundary, with a massive holly hedge as a background. This bed is wide enough to accommodate a broad path through its center and length. On either side grow summer-blooming magnolias (*M.* × *Wiesneri* has gorgeous highly scented flowers), stewartias, and davidias (the dove tree). Here are featured a *Cornus controversa,* with its striking reddish foliage and purple-red winter stems, and a *Franklinia alatamaha,* with its white summer flowers and vivid autumn foliage. For winter scent and color are varieties of witch hazel; for spring, drifts of dogtooth violets, *Erythronium revolution* 'White Beauty', and miniature *Iris cristata.* Summer is colorful with lavender, *Hypericum patulum* 'Hidcote', and *Crocosmia masoniorum,* and for autumn color there are various fothergillas. In the more shaded areas are many rhododendrons, and I have seeded *Erythronium revolution* 'Pink Beauty' and *Gentiana asclepiadea* throughout this area. Casting much shade here are three *Davidia involucrata* 'Vilmorin', with striking white bracts, and towering above them a *Sequoiadendron giganteum,* planted over forty years ago and now over one hundred feet tall.

A Cedrus atlantica glauca pendula *in the entry court and kiwi vine (*Actinidia chinensis) *over the door.*

Around its massive trunk is a deep collar of *Galanthus elwesii,* a tall, handsome snowdrop that makes a dramatic picture in February.

Our driveway, to the east of this area, is edged with Belgian cobblestones brought here as ballast in sailing ships years ago. The guest house, the original house in which we lived, is near by. This has its own small garden and surrounding it is the "Magnoliary." The *Magnolia campbellii* came from England as a small slip on its own roots and took thirty-five years to bloom. Now the pollen from it goes to hybridizers. Here in this environment of open shade grow lilies, favorites of mine. Lilies may not "toil or spin," but this does not apply to those who grow them! Also growing among the magnolias are corylopsis in several varieties and *Disanthus cercidifolius.* The former, a shrub used frequently in England, gives a welcome burst of primrose yellow tassels in spring. The latter, also known as the Katsura tree, gives a stained-glass splendor to the autumn. I prize them both.

One of the features of our house and garden is the large partially covered terrace facing southwest. At the south end is a pool with massive rocks coming down a slope to the water's surface. This, perhaps, is the most peaceful spot of the entire garden. Water contributes to this aura as it splashes gently from a small pool formed by a depression in a boulder to a much larger pool below. It is here on the terrace, refreshed by a cup of afternoon tea, that I often think of my garden past, present, and future.

In the early years we had, on occasion, skilled gardeners. Campbell, an Englishman, and Bruno, a Hungarian, were experienced gardeners of the old school. In recent years, we have had part-time help, young men and women, some eager, and some even very interested. The fact is, if my husband and I did not spend the major portion of our time in the garden, it could not exist as it is. I suspect John does it out of love for me, but he also loves to design and build. I work in the garden because I love planting, weeding, pruning, and propagating. I am most happy on my hands and knees working in the soil, carrying out an idea. I welcome visitors and gardening groups. Many professional growers visit the garden regularly, and I encourage them to take cuttings and seeds; I feel the fruits of my labor are being shared.

I have only included here those trees, shrubs, and plants I felt might be of particular interest. As with every gardener, I have my favorites among the more familiar varieties of plants. While I have not included these, they nonetheless play an important role in the design of the garden. I feel strongly a garden should not, indeed cannot, be static. Nowhere is this more true than in our area. Here growth can be extremely vigorous, and yet an occasional winter ice storm will wreak great havoc. I have had many long-cherished treasures annihilated, and so of necessity I have adapted a gardening philosophy of flexibility and change. I am as concerned with the form, structure, and overall design of a garden as I am with its contents. The placement of a tree or plant is as important to me as the plant itself. I like to think of my garden as a painting — which I hope never to finish.

In this detail of the rock garden the red spikes of Imperata cylindrica rubra *appear to the left of the dwarf cedar of Lebanon and gray* Euryops acraeus *to the right. The dwarf conifer beyond is* Cryptomeria japonica elegans nana *and the yellow-and-pink striped grass is* Halsonechloa macra albo-aurea.

Maureen Ruettgers

CARLISLE, MASSACHUSETTS

Polly's garden, with a miniature bee skep surrounded by asters and clumps of dianthus.

I GREW UP in a country garden in Michigan helping my mother with the rituals of preparing, seeding, and planting. But it wasn't until I married and moved again to a country setting that I once more became absorbed in gardening. After several years of planting too much and too close, I slowed down and began to focus on herb cultivation. I joined the Herb Society of America in 1975. This organization encourages sharing of knowledge and plant material. At monthly meetings, members bring baskets filled with seedlings, produce, or new cultivars to exchange. My entire allium border can be traced back to a 1930s' division from a founding member's garden.

Another great influence has been my friendship with Mary Milligan, which began fifteen years ago with my first visit to her home in Harvard, Massachusetts. As I entered her kitchen, I saw every spare space filled with plants and jars of herbs and spices; strings of shallots and garlic, woven together with willow bark, were dangling from the ceiling; herbs and grated peel of lemons and limes were drying on towels on the counter, and there were mortars and pestles of every size. From a big picture window I could see curved terraces spilling over with herbs. Later as we walked there she stopped to pick snippets to give me to take home to root. Now she no longer has a garden of her own, so she helps me with mine.

When we found our eighteenth-century New England saltbox in 1979, the main attraction wasn't the house or its age, but the greenhouse and drying rooms on the property. I learned that they had been built by the previous owner, James A. Patch, to grow and dry a superior medical grade of foxgloves (*Digitalis purpurea*) when imports of it were cut off by World War II. He developed a steam-heating system that sent a flow of warm air through the drying racks and kept the leaves at the potency required by federal drug standards.

The house faces south to capture the warmth of the winter sun. From old photographs I learned that the two parallel beds that lead to the stone entry had contained lupines and peonies, but I wanted plants that would always look fresh. My husband's tenth-anniversary gift was a garden trip to England; there I saw Sissinghurst, and I decided to borrow an idea from Vita Sackville-West's celebrated white garden. Only the soft silver of lamb's ears (*Stachys lanata*) and lavender cotton (*Santolina*) now fill the entry beds. And in their fourth year the plants already give the cool, refreshing effect I sought.

In the foreground is the narrow herb display garden, with American burnet, flax, and wooly thyme surrounded by the soft silver of lamb's ear. Beyond are the greenhouse and cutting gardens.

The old back garden was a jungle of weeds, woodbine, and tired perennials. I was pregnant that first fall and my husband still reminds me that I looked like a Japanese Buddha as I sat crosslegged madly pulling out miscellaneous plants. With Abigail soon to arrive, Polly five, and Christopher four, my major consideration was to use low-maintenance plants in the cleared ground, to which I had added manure, compost, and bonemeal. And I wasn't used to gardening in the filtered light created by a stand of mature oaks here. Fortunately Mary Milligan came to my rescue with epimediums, angelica, sweet cicely, and ribbon grass. She was determined that sweet woodruff would cover any bare spots, and we enjoy sprigs of it in May wine and for bouquets that smell of new-mown hay. Mary also solved the problem of the poison ivy in the old back beds. We did not want to spray because of our young children, so she had us gather stacks of old newspapers and pile them thickly over the problem area. A topdressing of straw, compost, and soil followed, and we were able to safely plant the area. The poison ivy has not returned and in its place is a thriving hedge of *Ilex crenata* 'Compacta'. In addition to Mary, my neighbor who has a nursery of field-grown perennials was another splendid resource. I spent hours touring her fields, digging Old World flowers.

By fall the drying room is filled with herbs, flowers, and wayside plant material. The drying frames for petals make for quick, arid drying conditions. Leaves for medicinal-grade digitalis were dried in this room during World War II.

My father built a large treehouse for his grandchildren in one of the oaks and Mary insisted that the children have a garden view on all sides. I chose hostas for low maintenance here, and my first was a gift from the daughter of Mary's own mentor, Frances Williams. Mrs. Williams, whose home was in Winchester, Massachusetts, was famous for her hosta collection and she distributed plants to the Arnold Arboretum and to the Oxford Botanic Garden in England. One of the most admired of the Oxford specimens was named for her, *Hosta sieboldiana* 'Frances Williams'. This was my gift, and it is especially lovely when dew is caught in the deep corrugations of its yellow-margined leaves.

An early project was the kitchen garden. My husband and I enjoy cooking with herbs and like to have them within easy reach. We set an old orchard ladder on the edge of the stone wall sloping down to the back lawn, and the rungs made easy dividers for chervil, rosemary, tarragon, thymes, parsley, and burnet. Caraway, thyme and alpine plants cling to the sides of the steps that descend through the stone wall, and my children can't resist running their hands over them.

The next task was to create a place for my personal collection of choice specimen herbs. I needed an area that would accommodate many plants and allow me to experiment with subtle combinations of color and texture. My husband built a fifty-foot-long raised bed, quite narrow so each plant was in easy reach. Ornamental alliums blend with lavenders, dwarf sage, and cool pink and blue *Salvia viridis*. Hops, American burnet, flax, anchusa, and orris root fill this garden. Everyone helped with the labeling, so enthusiastically that they even labeled our *Canoeus aluminus* and *Quercus forte alba* — our canoe and treehouse.

The main garden is the working garden. It holds Polly's plants for potpourri, mine for wreath-making, and my husband's vegetables. Ten square plots and four large rectangular ones were built to simplify crop rotation. The colorful center square belongs to Polly. All her plant choices were selected from Park's and Burpee's seed catalogues. She took cuttings of rosemary and seeded the others in trays in the greenhouse. She fills the center with plants of a geranium appropriately named 'Pretty Polly'. Her tiny sundial is surrounded by rosemary, lemon verbena and *Phlox drummondii*. A traditional bee skep nestles among clumps of dianthus and asters. Two pineapple-scented sages face each other to balance the garden. It is interesting to note her formal approach, so different from my casual style.

Our son Christopher, a year younger than Polly, grows pumpkins, parsley, peas, carrots, and peppers. He chooses what he likes to eat and can sell quickly at his small roadside stand, which he shares with his sister. Polly makes the signs to hold up, Chris gets into his Colonial Minuteman costume, and the sale is on! Their knowledge of supply and demand is already far greater than mine.

In spring we make plans for the squares in the cutting garden and set it up with bark mulch paths so the children do not tramp on each other's spaces. The late summer and fall is an active time when every family member is harvesting. My husband is preserving, Chris watches over his prize pumpkins, and the girls and I spend many hours going to and from the drying rooms. There are three separate drying rooms, the largest having the ovens where James Patch dried his digitalis leaves. The oven is divided into four sections, each with ten trays. Polly's potpourri material occupies one section and I use the remaining three. We fill all these with flowers and herbs from the cutting beds before October frosts.

September and October are when most of my wreath-making is accomplished. I like to work with a combination of fresh and dried material with varying color and textures. I gather the blossoms of the same plant at different times to acquire material with delicate gradations. All the bases for the wreaths are made from artemisia or garden sage. I bend the stems when they are still supple to form the chosen shape, then secure them by twining button or carpet thread around the shapes. Often I choose materials from the drying barn and the cutting garden, arranging them in a bouquet, and if they blend nicely together, I know they will work in a wreath. The possible combinations of flowers and herbs is endless, making each wreath unique. Weaving them together is similar to the way I plant my garden, with subtle color changes and different plant textures side by side.

On long summer days I like to rise at 5:30 A.M. and spend time in the garden before anyone else is about. The quiet time is precious for planning and taking notes for the day's tasks. Eventually, my garden may become more intricate and formal, but its simplicity is very workable with my young family.

Looking toward the eighteenth-century farmhouse and the drying rooms. The petals of the cosmos in the foreground turn a very deep red when dried and are used in potpourri. Beyond is a superior selection of French tarragon, which finds its way to some of the Boston area's finest French restaurants.

Lorrie Otto

MILWAUKEE, WISCONSIN

A six-foot-high cup plant seen through the kitchen window. Birds and insects drink the liquid that collects in the hollow formed where the leaf meets the stem.

MY GLORIOUS GARDEN is just perfect for me, and it measures up to the aesthetic and environmental standards that I care about passionately.

Its summer appearance is unusual for a suburban yard. Then slender perennial sunflowers and high wands of *Coreopsis tripteris* along with square-stemmed cup plants and other silphiums tower over my head. Milkweeds and Joe Pyes add dusky pinks to these sunny yellows. These forms are knit together by winged activity, pollinating insects, especially butterflies — monarchs, vanessas, swallowtails and fritillaries. As seeds form, goldfinches and chickadees add song and movement. In late afternoon bumblebees are still active but are replaced by beautiful moths as the evening progresses. The entire yard is my garden, with half an acre in trees and shrubs and the other half-acre in meadow and prairie.

Spring here is as beautiful as romantic love songs proclaim it to be. In shady patches wild geraniums are the dominant species, among the clones of ginger, bloodroot, assorted anemones, various violets, May apples and meadow rues under trees and shrubs. Trilliums and hepaticas find their places too. Where the sun shines in late spring, the wild roses, blue baptisias, and irises announce to my neighbors that the prairie show is beginning. In September, the asters and *Physostegia* echo the earlier pastel hues. White rounds of boneset, yarrow, and *Aster umbellatus* change the rhythm, while the purple and gold of asters and solidago join in a final crescendo. These are the colors the American poets first proclaimed for their country's autumn. Ours is the aster/goldenrod continent of the world. We have seventy-five of each species, while Europe only has three of goldenrods and a few native asters.

This symphony of color, form, and texture enable my garden to pass its first test, that of being satisfying aesthetically. The second test is, "Does it belong in this part of America?" In my neighborhood Norway spruces are the planted-pest species — alien and so numerous that they form a monoculture inviting insect infestation. Each year I remove one of my sixty-foot-tall trees and extend a prairie planting into that vacated space.

The eastern deciduous forest and the western prairie meet in Wisconsin. Often settlers found oak savannas — widely dispersed oak trees with prairie flowers and

grasses as the ground cover between them. The Nature Conservancy has preserved remnants of such lands, like the Chiwaukee Prairie along Lake Michigan at the Illinois–Wisconsin border.

I was introduced to prairie when I was a very young girl. My grandmother was an enthusiastic gardener, cultivating beds of moss roses and borders of flax along with poppy and lily gardens. Oddly, though, when she started me on my way with plants, she gave me an Easter basket and we hiked to the railroad tracks to gather shooting stars and pasque flowers, which she helped me transplant into the center of an old tire. I remember the orange puccoon that was too difficult to dig. She referred to it as "stone seed." Fifty years later I learned that this plant's botanical name, *Lithospermum,* translates to "stone seed." My sister, cousins, and I built thicket wigwams in the center of Grandma's vegetable garden. We could have been playing in real Indian country if only someone had told us to move our camp into the growth along the edges of the pastures.

In 1970 those misty memories came into focus during the Earth Day programs in Madison, Wisconsin, where I attended a prairie conference that dramat-

A late summer spectacle of three kinds of perennial sunflowers massed between clumps of gray-headed coneflowers in the foreground and stands of cupflowers in the rear of plantings along the entry drive.

ically changed my landscaping ideas. Those "weeds" of my childhood that were burned each spring along roads and railroad tracks were now threatened with extinction, along with the bird and insect life that they supported. Surely the only place left for a refuge would be in suburban yards where personal arboretums and insect zoos might someday develop into substantial restorations. We need places where caterpillars can feed, where fireflies can live, and where birds can find food and shelter. If enough of us could do this we could help maintain the gene bank of biological diversity. As children we all heard the story of the Ark, but few of us understand that if we care about people we must also care for the organisms that make our soil, clean our air, and purify our water. Politicians seldom seem to understand this, but surely gardeners should be able to.

The third criterion for judging my garden may well be how it affects the rest of the earth. It appears to be the American way to arrive ignorant into a new landscape, to denude it and replace it with a hodgepodge from other climates and even other countries, and then to squander energy to artificially maintain the vegetation. Today the application of chemicals to grow ornamentals is surely unconscionable. Nitrogen fertilizer requires finite resources, usually natural gas

Pink and white shooting stars, yellow hoary puccoon, and purple bird's-foot violets are among the two dozen varieties of native plants in bloom on Memorial Day in the Chiwaukee Prairie.

COLLECTORS AND SPECIALISTS

The winter menu for local wildlife includes seed heads of the pale purple coneflower, Canada wild rye, Black-eyed Susans, and (right) Brown-eyed Susans.

and petroleum. Phosphate mining deals Florida a horrendous environmental insult even as we haul our precious leaves to dumps where the phosphorus is not merely wasted but is then carried along waterways to destroy ever more life! Herbicides and insecticides break delicate food chains, hence none can be considered "safe." Also, to use them makes us part of the toxic waste conspiracy. My yard grows naturally with its diversity of native plants protecting themselves and replacing their losses. Moreover, because it is undisturbed, more soil is created there. The garden also has a positive effect on a greater environment. It is the first flush of rainwater running off roofs, drives, and lawns that carries so much lead and other pollutants to our streams and lakes. So I have created "submersible gardens," low spots that trap the water until the contaminants can filter out. Here I encourage plants like creeping moneywort (*Lysimachia nummularia*), swamp buttercup, and iris, which adapt well to periodic flooding.

Another test I apply when judging my garden is how it thrives without using any of our drinking water. Decorated rain barrels store the water I need for transplanting; the rest of the time the flowers are dependent on our thirty-four inches of yearly rainfall. When the photographs were taken to accompany this article, Wisconsin was suffering in a drought. My prairie plants were unaffected because of their deep root systems, and their phototropic or hairy or wax-coated or rolled or "venetian blind" leaves — such devices which have evolved over thousands of years in response to the burning sun and desiccating winds in the prairies.

My property reflects a sense of place because the plantings identify it as Midwest. It also sustains interest through the seasons. Wisconsin's first snowfall often arrives in November. The clay soil north of Milwaukee is usually heavy with autumn moisture. Storms sweep in and snow drifts among my winter bouquets.

Juncos feed under the finches and siskins as they scatter seeds from the stems of the dried forbs and grasses. The gray-headed coneflower (*Ratibida pinnata*) gives a staccato pulse in all kinds of weather. The purple coneflowers, with the largest seed heads of their family, have a hedgehog appearance that explains their botanical name of *Echinacea purpurea*. The orbs of black-eyed Susan (*Rudbeckia hirta*) are smudges against the snow, while their taller sisters, *R. triloba,* have the smallest balls at the ends of their finer branches. Wet snow storms adorn all of them with delightful white stocking caps. Rigid goldenrods (*Solidago rigida*) and the flat-topped asters are as pretty with their sepals of snow as they were with their petals of color.

Birds gather more than seeds. Often the dry flower stems quiver as feathered creatures explore for dormant insects. On the most bitter of winter days, an insectivorous shrew will give startling life to the area as it darts from hole to hole in the snow. Always, the mowed lawns beyond my yard appear so naked, bleak, cruel . . . absent of all life. Then I think of how wonderful my garden must look to new birds as they fly overhead at any time of the year.

I should emphasize that I sit in judgment only of my own garden. Other people's gardens are wonderful fairylands which I enjoy through their eyes and do not grade environmentally as I do my own. For my part it pleases me enormously that I have designed a yard in harmony with the natural world. For me that kind of beauty has no equal and it is the final, most important reason for the garden that nestles around my little chalet in Midwest America.

The south front of the house in late May with foundation plantings of pin cherry (Prunus pennsylvanica), *thimble berry* (Rubus ordoratus), *iris and peonies, and an American hazlenut at the corner. Wild geraniums flower among ground covers of strawberries, Jacob's ladder and shooting stars. Downspouts channel rainwater off the roof into storage barrels.*

THE GARDEN OF

Elisabeth C. Miller

SEATTLE, WASHINGTON

A Korean dogwood (Cornus kousa) *in full bloom above ferns,* Dryopteris erythrosorus *(center) and a northwest native deerfern* (Blechnum spicant).

W E ARE SITUATED on the banks of Puget Sound facing the Olympic Mountain Range. On a clear day the garden becomes the foreground of a spectacular view of the snow-capped mountains directly across the water. An impressive backdrop is provided by a 150-year-old forest of Douglas firs, cedars, hemlocks, madronas, maples, and dogwoods. The Northwest is well known for its inclement weather, but storms, white-capped waves, clouds, and even gray days have their own beauty. Our house has many windows from which we can enjoy these views with indoor comfort.

Our four-acre site provides a variety of exposures and horticultural conditions, from woodland to arid. The intensively developed garden features four thousand different plant species endemic to thirty-five countries, from the arctic to tropical regions, which are unified by the extensive use of Northwest natives. But I don't consider it a collector's garden, since the so-called collections are interspersed throughout the landscape. Rock garden plants, for example, are favorites, but rather than create a specialized area, I have used them throughout with the occasional outcroppings of rock. In its entirety, I see the garden as a single plant with an intermingling root system.

The garden descends steeply from a wooded area to the residence and onwards to the Sound. To hold the soil we have used aged logs and many tons of weathered granite, all of which have been collected from our mountains by truck and crane — at considerable expense. One log in particular I refer to as my "mink." These have been sited so deeply in the ground that no one is the wiser except the plants, which enjoy the resulting cool root runs, friable soil, and increased water retention on the upper sides of log or rock.

The design of the garden is informal and is viewed from wandering paths. In developing additional paths recently it occurred to me that setting them a foot or more below the existing ground level would give a pleasant feeling. I liked the effect and am planning to deepen all the paths.

When we built our house years ago, I had no particular interest in gardening and was virtually unaware of either daffodils or dandelions. But having majored in art, I began to see texture, form, and color in foliage, bark, and flowers. That settled it. I began to compose pictures, perhaps placing a pendulous conifer to

COLLECTORS AND SPECIALISTS

cascade over a boulder, or a blue-foliaged shrub to complement the blue needles of the *candescens* variety of the Colorado white fir. Right now, as the *Eucryphia* × *nymansensis* are bursting with the beauty of their white camellialike flowers, it occurs to me that I should transplant the *Kirengeshoma palmata* with its fall-blooming, yellow tubular waxy flowers to enhance the same area.

A number of the plant combinations that delight me were strictly accidental. Little did I know that the blue flowers of a *Clematis macropetala* climbing through a golden rain tree (*Koelreuteria paniculata*) would appear simultaneously with the tree's young red-tinted foliage. The beautiful range of fall colors of *Disanthus cercidifolius* are especially lovely when mingling with the blue branches of the Japanese white pine (*Pinus parviflora* 'Glauca'). As the plant material matures, the garden more and more takes on the aspect of a mosaic of texture, form, and color that changes constantly through the year.

I have usually been tempted by choice forms of species both difficult to acquire and challenging to grow. My plants have come from round the globe and from such great plantsmen as Sir Henry H. Hillier, Ted and Mary Grieg, Dr. E. H. Lohbrunner, and Carl S. English, Jr.

With "difficult" plants, I think our greatest hazard is sudden and extreme fluctuation of weather; in the midst of a long, cloudy, and cool spring, a sudden day of full sun and high temperatures can abruptly attack and burn the new foliage. But we basically have a favorable climate, and with protection from the dehydrating winds and an appropriate site (the microclimates seem to vary every ten feet), many unlikely and tender species can thrive. Close planting of ground covers also helps, with companion root systems seeming to enhance biological activity within the soil.

There was much to learn from the wicked freeze of 1955, which occurred after an unusually warm and wet fall that had caused untimely new growth. Our large-leaved tropical rhododendrons were killed to the ground. Mournfully, but with hope in my heart, I staked the sites and was amazed to see new growth appear at ground level two years later, followed by rapid renewal. Five years later another freeze cut them back, but not to the ground, and since then they have come through freezes untouched. Acclimatization?

An advantage of growing species rather than hybrids is that the former require less maintenance. What is required is an understanding of the plant's needs for soil conditions. Pipsissewa (*Chimaphila menziesii*) needs the natural decomposition of fallen fir needles, so it is planted where it gets this. I sometimes wonder just who is creating the landscape, the plants or me. One of the greatest gifts of the garden is clumps of Indian pipe (*Monotropa uniflora*, a member of the *Ericaceae* family that has no chlorophyll). This is beyond the ability of man to establish and appears when and if it chooses.

A recent surprise was provided by our prostrate Korean fir, which after twenty-five years has suddenly borne tight clusters of small cones standing erectly along its branches. The authorities have it that this form does not bear cones! What a frustration to be responsible as an authority for the behavior of plant species. Many of our plants show how plants endemic to one climate or soil or

An Archtostasphylos manzanita *blooms above the ground covers* Indigofera incarnata, Ceratostigma plumbaginoides *and an unusual epimedium* (E. perralderianum) *(far right).*

The bright fall foliage of Acer aconitifolium *(above) and* Fothergilla monticola *(middle) stand out in a hillside collection of uncommon plants that also includes the golden* Metasequoia sempervirens albo-spica, *the graceful* Juniperus chinensis 'White Cloud' *(lower right), and the* Tsuga canadensis jenkinsii *(upper left).*

The Rhododendron forestii repens *is a single fifty-year-old plant interplanted with* Galax aphylla. *In the foreground is an unnamed dwarf New Zealand hebe.*

*A handsome fern (*Osmunda japonica*) on the step above a rare white-flowering* Indigofera decora alba, *a tender evergreen that behaves as a deciduous plant in the Miller garden.*

humidity zone can adapt to another. They may take their own time and moderate some characteristic, such as habit of growth or leaf size, and thus become difficult to recognize. Others change from evergreen to deciduous, as for example, the beautiful and tender evergreen *Indigofera decora* var. *alba* from Japan. For us it acts as a deciduous plant and is becoming almost invasive. Currently I am challenging groups of tropical Vireya rhododendrons to grow among some hardier evergreen shrubs for protection. This will be a future chapter. I'm also looking forward to the maturation of *Pseudowintera colorata*, which I acquired from Hillier's Nursery in England. Having never seen a full-grown specimen, I am watching with interest. The evergreen foliage is softly multicolored with red edging.

The interest that wildlife gives the garden is good reason for trusting nature's biological insect control instead of spraying. Some of the animal and bird species have designated their own territory and show marked curiosity when I am planting or just fussing around. Chipmunks have home-based on our extensively planted terrace, and as one guest commented, "They definitely do *not* like garden tours!"

The birds are also great plantsmen. It seems that the species *Fagus sylvatica*

The intermingling of shrubs like Leucothoe keiskii *and* Rhododendron pentaphyllum, *its leaves outlined in red, and ground covers like* Potentilla nitida 'Fireflame' *and the little-leaved northwest native* Gaultheria procumbens *is characteristic of plantings in the garden.*

forma *atropunicea* (copper beech, and not to be confused with purple beech) produces few viable seeds and thus is not a practical tree for nurseries. But we find them planted prodigiously here and there in the garden, and after several years I pot them up and give them to friends.

During the past ten years I have used ferns much more prominently. The very strong pattern of evergreen *Blechnum tabulare* from South Africa adds a bold accent. The fronds are heavy, leathery, and these rust-colored fertile fronds are a conversation piece as well as being a handsome companion to the large leathery-foliaged rhododendrons, with their rust-colored indumentum. The evergreen *Poly-podium* varieties also have a strong pattern, with variety *scouleri* growing to one and a half feet, and it too is a handsome addition. I am so fond of this fern I had a gold brooch made which depicts both sides of a frond, and the design is similar to an herbarium specimen. I have used many of the smaller ferns, such as the *Woodsia* and *Ceterach officinalis,* with the rock outcroppings. The diminutive dwarf forms, which vary from five inches to twelve inches, of *Adiantum pedatum aleu-ticum* (maidenhair fern) are used with choice perennials, and a variety of charming evergreen Japanese ferns graces the ground covers surrounding larger ornamentals.

I have enjoyed using the garden extensively for educational tours for community college horticultural classes, University of Washington landscape classes, and numerous garden clubs. Two comments I treasure, from people who I felt understood the philosophy of our garden, are those of Russell Page, who inscribed *The Education of a Gardener,* "To Betty — from an author goggle-eyed with admiration and enchanted with the most erudite forest floor to be seen anywhere", and of Dr. René Dubos, who autographed his book *A God Within,* "To Betty — and to the god within her garden."

Sally MacBride

WOODSIDE, CALIFORNIA

OMEWHERE I once read never try to have a garden in an old orchard or near a creek, and, idly, I wondered why not. Now I know!

Twenty-five years ago we acquired three acres in an old apple orchard beside a creek, built our house, and started a garden. The deer who were accustomed to coming for windfalls found welcome additions to their diet in our newly planted garden. The gophers and moles who lived near the creek were happy to move up in the world into our newly watered areas, especially the lawns. The rabbits came later, when the shrubbery had grown sufficiently to afford them protection from our cats. In addition to these hazards, sandstone underlay much of our heavy clay. An old-timer told us that dynamite had to be used eighty years earlier to dig the holes for the apple trees. All these factors had their impact on our garden. We learned to make compost in quantity, plant in wire, mulch, and above all, to prepare the soil *very* well before planting. It's not all bad to have obstacles to overcome.

Because our land was virtually flat we decided to build berms — or mounds, as I call them — in front of the house to create interest, privacy, and, most essential, good drainage. While berms are usually utilitarian, they need not appear so. Nor is creating a berm a difficult task, but it does require large amounts of soil and soil amendments. Our method was to set aside all the topsoil collected from digging the foundations of the house. Then we commenced to build up the mounds with woody cuttings, leaves, pine needles, and soil from planting holes. Before the fall rains began we added the topsoil and copious amounts of coarse wood shavings and manure. Next we rototilled sand and firbark into the top foot. Lastly we raked and raked until the berms were the approximate shape we wanted and had contours that pleased the eye. Then we let the whole thing sit through the winter. A fair amount of settling took place, but this was remedied in the spring with more materials and more raking. Only then was it safe to start planting, and since the contours are gentle, erosion was minimal as the planting took hold. The occasional judicious placement of a large rock or boulder helps maintain the slope and can be an attractive addition. We should have, but did not, put in the necessary drainage during construction and we had to add drainage tiles later. But now, buried in gravel trenches covered with large river-washed stones, they lead to the creek. Only we know what lies beneath this ornamental feature.

Chinese wisteria festoons the moongate (opposite) and an antique Chinese tile mounted on the fence (above). More curves are seen in the clipped myrtle hedges and the Dutch holly beyond the entrance.

There are five major mounds and they hold plants from many parts of the world. From California there are prostrate manzanitas (*Arctostaphylos* × 'Emerald Carpet' and 'Woods Compact') with pink heathlike flowers in winter and spring and red berries in summer and fall. Another native, the prostrate wild lilac (*Ceanothus gloriosus*), is covered with light blue flowers in the spring. From New Zealand there is a low-mounding ground cover, *Myoporum parvifolium*, with bright green feathery foliage and pink or white flowers sporadically all year. The low-growing Australian fuchsia cultivars (*Correa* × 'Carmine Bells' and 'Ivory Bells') have pointed gray-green leaves and deep pink or white inch-long pendant bell-shaped flowers all fall and winter. From the Mediterranean, the sun roses (*Helianthemum nummularium* hybrids) and rockroses (*Cistus corbariensis* and × 'Doris Hibberson') flower profusely in spring and again in summer if cut back and watered. A shrubby manzanita (*Arctostaphylos hookeri*) adds height in plantings along the tops of the two largest mounds. An unnamed hebe with pointed lavender flower spikes in May cascades down the slope beneath a flowering crab.

Some new experimental plantings are showing promise — *Kunzea pomifera* from Australia, very prostrate with tiny light green leaves and edible purplish fruit;

*Mats of campanulas, deep blue lithodora, and white candytuft carpet the shrub beds around the terrace. In the foreground a fragrant Mexican orange (*Choysia ternata*).*

a *Grevillea alpina* cultivar with lacy gray foliage and bright red flowers and two low-sprawling leptospermums (*L. scoparium* 'Pink Cascade' and *L. humifusum*). Alas, the heavenly blue *Dampierra diversifolia* from Australia merely survives but does not thrive.

Ornamental trees here include *Parrotia persica* and *Ginkgo biloba* for their brilliant yellow fall color; the bead tree (*Melia azedarach*) with its spring clusters of violet flowers and yellow fruit (the beads) in the fall, and the rosy summer-blooming crape myrtle. The Chinese tallow tree (*Sapium sebiferum*), Japanese black pine, and several Japanese maples and flowering crabs combine to give a somewhat oriental effect to the whole area.

The most "Japanese" garden was once just beyond the largest mound. It began as a wide informal pathway to the tennis court and was planted in dichondra. It was meant to look like a stream complete with little islands and carefully placed rocks. The mounds curving up on either side were ideal for rock garden plants and shrublets. It was really very charming. But after several years of having the rabbits eat the dichondra, the cold blacken it, and heavy rains turn the path into a real stream, we re-engineered the drainage and substituted a soft beige gravel for the dichondra — and we have never regretted it. Now a progression of miniature bulbs, dwarf spireas and daphnes, and the bright flowers of silenes and campanulas give it the look of an alpine meadow through spring, summer, and fall. Grape hyacinths and miniature daffodils have escaped into the gravel and the whole effect is very satisfying.

The swimming pool is on the south side of the house and the daffodil garden alongside it has an unusual design. The area is partially paved with large adobe blocks and the daffodils grow in large patches in randomly scattered unpaved pockets. The bloom is quite spectacular and the paving keeps the flowers from becoming muddy and bedraggled in the rain. Every other year we dig up the bulbs, move them into the field and plant new ones in their stead. A colorful swatch beyond the paving is created by a wide bed filled with the warm pastels of alstroemerias, sparaxis, and apricot watsonias in late spring. After these southern hemisphere bulbs finish, the summer blues of agapanthus, Chinese plumbago and caryopteris offer a cooler effect.

The back of the house faces west toward the creek that bounds our property. An arbor extends across the width of the house shading the terrace below from the afternoon sun. The beds here are planted mostly with a variety of ferns, from the Tasmanian tree fern to miniature maidenhairs. Two beautiful camellias, the double pink 'Tiffany' and the watermelon red 'Captain Rawes', are spectacular in the spring and can be enjoyed through the drawing room windows. At the north end of the terrace we planted three silk trees (*Albizia julibrissin*). They are beautiful in summer and the hummingbirds love their pink flowers, but they were a mistake. They are both greedy and dirty. In time, as the Japanese maples and lacebark trees (*Hoheria populnea*) grow larger, we will remove them.

The beds ringing the terrace are "mixed," with shrubs for year-round backing. Chinese witch hazel (*Loropetalum chinense*) is an evergreen medium-sized shrub with typical white witch hazel flowers. The Mexican orange (*Choiysa ternata*) has

A late winter view of the berm that screens the front of the house. One wing of the U-shaped house can be seen. In the foreground is the beginning of the path to the tennis court.

A sculpted hippopotamus surrounded by Saxifrage primuloides.

fragrant white flowers and aromatic foliage. Perennial favorites here are an outstanding cultivar of English lavender, 'Twickel Purple', more akin to French or Spanish lavender; Australian bluebell (*Sollya heterophylla*) and blue mist (*Caryopteris × clandonensis*). They are underplanted with campanulas, the "true" geraniums (*sanguineum, pratense, cinereum*), gentians, dianthus hybrids, *Lithodora diffusa* 'Heavenly Blue' and the geranium relative *Erodium chamaedryoides*. There are also a number of unusual little spring bulbs — corn lilies (*Ixia*), *Gladiolus tristis* with a heavenly evening fragrance, and *Lapeirousia laxa* with white or coral blooms resembling a tiny gladiola. The lily family is represented by two members with bright blue flowers, *Aristea thyrsiflora* and *Pasithea caerulea*. Something unusual is blooming most of the year.

Two of the pleasantest aspects of the creek bank are a bed of parma violets, which bloom joyously and fragrantly all spring, and the aromatic festoons of the old musk and banksia roses, which have climbed into the oaks and pines here. Their perfume is everywhere in May. The working areas of the garden — lath house, potting shed, small glass house, and compost boxes — are on the north side of the house screened by a curving wooden fence festooned with wisteria and jasmine. The moon gate opening on the drive is the final oriental detail.

If I were to characterize my garden I would have to call it a collector's garden, for plants have been my great interest and joy. I like having unusual, rare, or new plant material and if I can make it happy I propagate it, use it in my garden, and give it to friends and fellow "plant nuts." I began by collecting flowering trees and shrubs, then I became enamored of native California plants, and then of unusual ground covers promising low maintenance. I had a "blue period" when I collected only blue flowers. Remnants of all these and other stages remain and are old friends and standbys. Most recently I discovered trough gardening, so far with mixed results. I particularly love the small aristocrats of the plant world — the *Lewisias, Ramondas, Haberleas* and *Gentianas* — but they are not particularly happy in this climate.

Each year we have new projects. A garden cannot be static; either it is going forward, developing and changing, or it declines. A garden that is not renewed will die of old age just like anything else. At the moment we are acquiring new and more elaborate fences; the beds along the creek bank are due for rehabilitation; and the tennis court planting is overgrown and needs replacement. The list is long and never gets any shorter. I put gardeners into two categories — those who own gardens and those who are owned by their gardens. We belong in the second group!

The curving path suggests a flowing stream. Foliage and flowers harmonize with the blues and grays of the stones.

COLLECTORS AND SPECIALISTS

Lurline Coonan

WOODSIDE, CALIFORNIA

Jasminum officinale *in full bloom.*

An Oregon white oak frames the view of the California meadows. 'George Taber' azaleas and blue felicia are in the beds along the path circling the garden.

O**UR PROPERTY** of thirty-two acres was originally part of Rancho las Pulgas, an old Spanish land grant. The countryside all around us is one of rolling grassy hills studded with native California oaks, the fields changing from deep green in winter and spring to a golden straw color in summer and fall. At the entrance is a small family orchard of persimmon and olive trees. From here a road winds across fields and two small creeks on its way to the house. The rural atmosphere is complete with cattle grazing in the fields.

The Pennsylvania-style Colonial house with its second-story overhang for defense against Indians fits comfortably into the western California landscape. After we bought the property in 1951, I began to adapt the already established garden to feature typical California plants and to add perennials that suit our climate and offer both winter and summer interest. Within the garden I have defined various areas with paths, fences, walls and hedges. Annuals and perennials bloom along the paths, and I have made areas for shrubs and cutting flowers as well as for vegetables and fruit trees. Birch, native oak, and a grove of redwoods border the garden and frame the view of the surrounding meadows.

The patterned entrance garden, square and formal, is particularly appropriate to the architecture of the house. It is enclosed by a picket fence covered with summerblooming jasmine (*Jasminum officinale*). Low clipped hedges of germander (*Teucrium chamaedrys*) or little-leaved euonymus (*E. microphylla*) edge the beds, which contain a spring display of *Primula malacoides, Cineraria grandifolia,* and a light blue pansy called 'Imperial'. For summer and fall this planting is changed to *Impatiens balsmina* and petunias.

My favorite features in the garden are the vines: the Concord grapes that run along the bottom of the second-story overhang on two sides of the house, the evergreen *Clematis armandii* growing up the outside chimney wall, and the wonderful wisterias, both floribunda (Japanese) and sinensis (Chinese), trained along the entire back overhang of the house.

In the southern and western sections of the gardens are lawns sloping gently away from the house toward planting beds along a circular path around the garden perimeter. Here I have placed lilacs, Indian hawthorn (*Raphiolepsis indica*), the soft lavender *Rhododendron* 'George Taber', variegated weigela, and the tall native fern

A fringe of wisteria on the back of the house.

Woodwardia fimbriata underplanted with ginger (*Asarum europaeum*) and lighted with the white, crocuslike flowers of the zephyr lily (*Zephyranthes candida*), which appear in May.

The formal rose garden is completely surrounded by a stone wall topped by a picket fence. The beds, divided by euonymus hedges, contain a large collection of roses, to which I frequently add. Iris of various colors give further interest to this garden. Since I am an enthusiastic flower arranger, I concentrate on floribunda roses rather than the hybrid teas. The floribundas can be picked in bud and will open in water, while I find that the hybrid teas have to be picked in nearly full bloom and therefore don't last as long. Among my favorites are the pink and yellow 'Little Darling', the yellow 'Circus', and the brilliant red-orange 'Olé'.

The patterned beds of the vegetable garden are outlined with green-and-white-striped society garlic. This garden is designed to make a lovely picture from the breakfast room window and to supply the household with vegetables. In the center is an old well covered with creeping ficus and surrounded by a low rock wall. There are pear trees and dwarf peach trees along the outer walls; the whole ensemble has a delightfully appetizing atmosphere.

Ranunculus fill the kitchen garden in April. Part of the circular center well can be seen at the left. Green-and-white-striped society garlic edges the center beds.

The fruit trees are placed principally at the entrance to the property, some twenty trees on either side of the road: olives, persimmons, apples, and pomegranates. The large harvest of scarlet persimmons looks beautiful during October and we and our neighbors are kept busy picking the olives, which are then brined in the old-country style for table use. The apricots are particularly delicious if we manage to collect them before the raccoons get to them. We have almond and fig trees and two varieties of lemon, Meyers and Eureka. All the family enjoys our fruit harvest.

During the summer we are away a great deal of time at our cattle ranch in Oregon so naturally I have become particularly interested in spring and fall colors. I have planted flowering dogwood, crabs, and cherries, and an eastern redbud.

Over the years I have managed to take care of the garden with the assistance of one full-time gardener, whose duties include propagation, planting, mowing, and, of course, the extensive watering so necessary during our arid summer months. As to my duties, I direct the planting and help with it. Being a dirt gardener I happily spend hours weeding, and I also spend much time pruning the shrubs and fruit trees.

The spring display of pansies in the rose garden. The roses are planted around the perimeter. Later, petunias will fill the box-edged parterres. A crab flowers in the background.

By midsummer the wisteria is a green swag along the side of the house. This view of the kitchen garden shows the geometry of walls, hedges, and paths. Yarrow along the path thrives on the summer heat.

My first real exposure to plant material was at my family's beautiful garden at the Filoli estate, since given to the National Trust. After my marriage, my interest in gardening continued, of course, until we came to our beautiful house and garden in Woodside. After perhaps ten years of going ahead on my own, I decided I needed some additional education in the field of horticulture. For two years I attended horticultural classes under the direction of Alex Graham at the College of San Mateo. This provided me with the background that I found to be of infinite value. Happily our gardener also attended classes, which has made us very compatible.

I am happy with my garden as it exists today, and confident that I can build on my experiences to continue to improve it. The garden is truly mine, and I believe that it gives the impression of being loved and lived in, as indeed it is.

COUNTRY GARDENS

The Garden of Hannah Wister

OLDWICK, NEW JERSEY

An orange trumpet vine in bloom over the entrance to the enclosed kitchen garden filled with flowers, fruit, and vegetables.

BOUT TWENTY-FIVE YEARS ago I decided to sell my Oldwick farm, keeping the highest fields, which were fairly flat, and to begin all over again. We picked the place for the house by standing on the roof of a truck to find the best view and settled on a spot that provided a panorama of about 180°.

The next order of business was to build the house. The question of design was solved by the discovery of an old farmhouse falling into decay on a factory lawn in Findern, some fifteen miles away. We loved it at first sight, this two-hundred-year-old dwelling. The factory manager was happy to get rid of it for $1000, so it was moved in pieces to the spot we had picked. Two small wings were added, one for the kitchen and one for the flower room.

Since the house faces south, the garden was laid out smack against the house on the east side, where it receives hours of sun. It is a true kitchen garden, the vegetables at hand for instant cooking. Nearest the house is the original garden, with four beds for spring vegetables separated by flagstone paths and with a sundial from my grandmother's garden in the middle. The beds are intensively cultivated in the French manner of closely planted vegetables. The French never waste an inch of space and don't give vegetables as much space as most Americans do. So we press the plants right up against each other. These beds are edged with clipped hedges of lavender and *Teucrium,* like beds we had seen in old gardens in Odessa, Maryland.

Later we enlarged the garden to about eighty feet square and had a fence built copying the decoration on the cornice of the house. The pickets swoop between pillars crowned with turned finials of French design and all are painted white to match the cornice of the yellow house. Our good friend Daniel Lindley was the garden architect.

The additional space gave room for flowers, fruit, and the more rampant vegetables. The new space is screened from the house by a dividing hedge of espaliered apple trees, which also form a backdrop for my roses. The hedge is about four feet tall and is lovely when in bloom. Beyond is a ten-foot-wide strip of grass and then two more beds of constantly changing vegetables. Our gardener Teo manages to have two crops of everything. We are away for July and August, so we need a spring and fall garden. He is a magician!

Everbearing raspberries which fruit in June and again from September until frost have a permanent spot in the garden. We rotate almost everything else. The tomatoes climb the fence with vigor, giving us a generous supply of tomato juice year round. Along the south fence we have narrow beds with currants and gooseberries. We have also made standard currant trees of which we are very proud and they have their own spot. Two dwarf pear trees near the center of the garden are all that remain of what I had hoped would be an allée of fruit trees — mirabelle, apricot, and apple. It didn't work.

Inside the east fence, the first flowers to bloom are the tree peonies given years ago by my beloved uncle, Jack Wister. The first flowers are the primroses, which we raise inside and then put out, pretending they've been there all along. Later perennials that do well are shasta daisies, columbine and penstemons. The annual zinnias, blue salvia, and marigolds for cutting in the fall are seeded or set out as small transplants in midsummer.

The garden has spread, much as we have tried to keep it confined by the picket fence. Somehow asparagras, strawberries, okra, rhubarb, and cutting flowers have been planted outside its limits. The walk-in cold frame provides delicious salad greens from the middle of April.

All these fruits, flowers, and vegetables grow happily together, and of course we are forever experimenting and changing. We are now trying standard lilacs after seeing them in Monet's garden at Giverny. And we have also tried to copy some of the grand Villandry patterns in miniature. It's never ending. . . .

A detail of the garden later in the season with the lavender in bloom and the standard currants in fruit. The more rampant vegetables grow in beds beyond the rose border. Young standard rosemaries and tuberoses are in pots.

Sugar snap peas and salad vegetables in the beds nearest the kitchen. A sundial marks the intersection of the paths in the earliest part of the garden.

COUNTRY GARDENS

Adele Lovett

PLEASANCE

LOCUST VALLEY, LONG ISLAND

The winter form of Stewartia pseudocamellia *is reflected by the pyramidally clipped yews.*

W E CALLED our property Pleasance, which is defined as "a small house or pavilion in the midst of gardens laid out for delight." We were thinking of our old age in building our small one-story house, and my objective for the gardens of delight was simple. I wanted to have as many flowers as possible so I could pick all year round for my house, my church, and my sick friends. I've therefore crowded in every flowering and berried tree and shrub that I like and that is hardy in our climate, as well as every perennial, annual, bulb, corm, and ground cover that I can grow, in all shades of pink from blush to deep rose. Except for an area of yellows at the service entrance and a blue-and-white border on the east side of the lawn, the colors are predominantly pinks.

I am happy to say that our vases are always full twelve months of the year. Thanks to a great variety of tiny fall- and winter-flowering iris and cyclamen, Christmas and Lenten roses, and all the tiny bulbs, especially crocus, scilla, snowdrops, and muscari, there is always something for the little vases. The big vases have handsome evergreens brightened with berried branches, red- and yellow-stemmed dogwood branches, or flowering sprays of forsythia, witch hazel, corylopsis, winter honeysuckle, Japanese quince, or rhododendrons which have been forced in a sunny window. We also bring in for a day or two, from the unheated glassed-in porch, an occasional potted camellia in full bloom.

We moved to Locust Valley and my father-in-law's big old house in 1937, after his death, and then began looking for a small place. Finally we decided to keep two and a half acres at the foot of the hill on his property and build our house there. I chose the location for its three beautiful old copper beech trees and a huge lavender-flowering rhododendron that is at least a hundred years old and thirty feet around. (It blooms on the 28th of May every year.)

On the day in 1939 that we broke ground for the house, my husband was called down to Washington by President Roosevelt; we were gone for fifteen years. So the house was built without me but managed to come out pretty well. Even as the house was rising I began my first project, screening the site, since we were completely exposed to the road. As soon as I returned to Long Island I continued the job of planting out the roadside and the view of the neighbors as

Only pink and white flowers are allowed in the secret garden alongside the bedroom windows.

A contemporary fox and a classical maiden haunt the woodland.

quickly as I could, with the cheapest things I could buy, six-foot-high hemlocks and three-foot-high rhododendrons, three for $1.50. They grew incredibly quickly and very soon formed a boundary around the whole property. In three years we no longer saw cars passing.

I also added a variety of flowering trees and shrubs alongside the boundary path that runs gently north to south. And then, a little at a time, I began to make a woodland area laced with small paths. It is planted with dogwoods (American and oriental), hollies, sorrel for its beautiful autumn foliage, Japanese tree lilacs, Cornelian cherry, the silver bell tree, benzoin, clethera, viburnums, and, at last count, some sixty-eight varieties of rhododendron and azaleas. They are all underplanted with wildflowers, bulbs, ferns and various kinds of ground covers.

In planning this place, two of the people who influenced me most were Constance Spry and Vita Sackville-West. Everything they suggested as desirable, I planted. I liked the idea of planting in drifts of single colors, because this makes it easier to pick flowers for arrangements. Constance got me interested in the old

French roses when I worked with her during the two years just before World War II when she had a shop in New York.

One firm idea in planting this property was that I never wanted to weed, and the only way to accomplish this was to have ground covers growing in every inch of open space. I researched the problem by flying up in 1943 to the property in Maine run by Beatrix Farrand, the great landscape architect, to study her enormous collection of ground covers, and I flew back to Washington the next day with a list of hundreds of names; I planted all of them and more. Now if there is a scrap of ground showing, I mulch heavily with leaf mold and very soon one of the ground covers will take over. Nothing could be more useful than the ordinary ajuga, which comes in many shades of foliage and flower color.

When we were still living in Washington there was a beautiful house on Dupont Circle I drove by regularly. One afternoon I discovered that the house I admired so much had been torn down (for the installation of streetcars on Connecticut Avenue) since I had passed it that morning. I left my car standing in the middle of Dupont Circle and ran to find the superintendent to ask what they had done with the magnificent columns that had flanked the front door and held up

Woodland plantings are composed along a network of paths.

the roof. They were out at his stoneyard by the railroad track, I was told. I went out there the next morning and told my story, that I had been trying to buy a wellhead for my garden but all the old Italian or French ones were hideously expensive. Instead I wanted to use a capital from one of the columns but supposed it would cost a fortune to get it to Long Island. To my joy I was told that since I am on the railroad, the shipping would cost only $30 and I could have the capital for another $30. When it arrived, half the village followed it up from the station, egging on the men dragging it. It was fiercely heavy and everyone had to help to lift it to its permanent foundation in my garden. That was quite an event.

When we came back here in 1954, I finished the picking garden, which is bordered on the east by my beloved old French roses. I began collecting them while we were still in Washington, living in the Shoreham Hotel. The hotel had trial beds of roses created by rosarians from all over the country to advertise their offerings. I checked them every day and made notes about the ones that bloomed best. One day I was on my hands and knees trying to find a plant label (which are always on the farthest side at the very bottom of a bush), when suddenly I saw two feet beside me and heard a voice asking if I would like some help. I looked up and saw a large name tag saying Robert Perkins of Jackson and Perkins. I got right up and told him about my plans. As a result I went to his nursery in Newark, New York, and bought all my roses. I still have them now forty years later.

I have also planted what I call a little secret garden alongside my bedroom. It is filled with small roses and other pink and white blooming plants. My blue-and-white border north of the secret garden has the bluest of the azaleas, 'Ramapo Hills' and 'Sterlington', blue-leaved hostas, hydrangeas, globe thistles, campanulas, catmint, and for annuals ageratum and lobelia 'Cambridge Blue'. I also have the beautiful summer-flowering rose-of-Sharon, an old-fashioned shrub that is usually a nasty pink except for this one, which is called 'Blue Boy'.

I planted entirely out of my allowance for groceries, so every week I would spend what was left over. I try to select everything when it is in bloom, and I always stop at little nurseries along the road and pick out anything interesting that is flowering. I have had a lot of fun and really now have a synoptic garden of desirable plants that will bloom in our climate.

Here at Pleasance I had to learn all over again, because I had always gardened in sunlight and sandy soil, and here I was in deepest shade with pure clay. Every time I dug the smallest hole I added masses of peat moss, and everything has increased luxuriantly. So much so that we have had to chop out, dig out, prune out, and give away much of what we overplanted. One year I asked my husband what he wanted for Christmas. He promptly replied: "A machete." "Whatever for?" I asked. "To hack my way through to the garage from the front door!"

I try to find special animal sculptures for the garden. My first was of a ground hog, which gave me the idea of having only the animals that live here. A rabbit and a hedgehog were easy to find, but a raccoon was another matter, so I commissioned Vicky Ward to make one. Dozens of them come to the bird feeder and eat every bit of seed. It takes them all night and I talk to them and they talk to

The wellhead created from the capital of a column that once graced a house on Dupont Circle in Washington, D.C.

The enormous Rhododendron roseum elegans *in full bloom at the end of May is at least a hundred years old.*

me. A little gray fox had its cub killed on the road and haunted the place until I had her taken to a reserve; so I had the fox made. Now I have asked for a great horned owl, which I think will be wonderful on a post behind the rhododendrons.

It certainly helps to have gardening friends, who tell you all kinds of tricks. One told me I should thin out the trees and let a little sun in, and then I could plant rhododendrons galore. George Rose brought me a little clump of maidenhair fern from his place in the Adirondacks and told me to put lime in the soil. It worked like a charm and now it is an enormous patch. Ferd Eberstadt helped me when I was having a terrible time with my clematis; he told me to shade the roots. (The cheapest way to do this is to turn a clay pot upside down, knock out the bottom, and pull the clematis plant through. I have never lost a clematis since.)

I'm always moving and changing things in the garden. I walk around six or seven times daily with some blue-painted stakes and put them where I want to rearrange something. And I always find something interesting going on.

THE GARDEN OF

Marie Aull

AULLWOOD, DAYTON, OHIO

I OFTEN THINK how little my husband and I had to do with the making of Aullwood. The glaciers that covered this part of Ohio formed the topography, creating contours of hills and valleys from the underlying limestone, carving the beds of the two little streams that meander through our thirty acres, and depositing the glacial till that nourishes our woodland. As the glaciers slowly retreated, the forests returned. Today there are over seventy varieties of native trees on the land, with oak, maple, beech, tulip, poplar, ash, sycamore, and Kentucky coffee trees dominating an understory of dogwood and redbud.

The average climate here is that of Zone 5, although temperatures have been known to go down to 20° below zero. Normally, we have about thirty-six inches of rain, pleasant weather in spring and fall, and summer temperatures ranging from 70° to 90°, with some spells of 95° weather.

Sixty years ago, when we came to live permanently in our small house in the woodland bordering the Stillwater River, our first task was to fence off the adjoining seventy acres of farm. Within a short time many native wild flowers germinated from seeds that had lain dormant during the previous period, when cattle grazed the land. We helped the process by buying replacements for plants that had disappeared. The tens of thousands of Virginia bluebells (*Mertensia virginica*) that for decades have covered our hillsides in late April are the progeny of a hundred plants we purchased. Our *Collinsia verna,* or Blue-eyed Mary, now growing in profusion, are the result of a happy discovery of a nearby colony that was about to be plowed under by a farmer enlarging his field. For the first two weeks in May, they give us some of our loveliest pictures, not only massed throughout the woodland, but also appearing in our long perennial border, undulating between the yellow daisylike flower of leopard's-bane (*Doronicum*), the early tree peonies, and the late daffodils. This scene has a backdrop of flowering crab and low shrubs of golden *Kerria japonica.*

Spring bulbs come to mind whenever one gardens in the shade, as we do, for the most part. For several years daffodils were my passion; they are still the dominant element in April, providing a month of spectacular bloom. Most of our shrubs sport an undercover of winter aconites and snowdrops, and the hillside in the front of the house is a mass of *Scilla siberica,* chionodoxa, puschkinia, and,

Leopard's-bane with Blue-eyed Mary.

Woodland swimming pool in glade of bluebells.

Drifts of bluebells (Mertensia virginica) *on the slope to the beech lawn.*

Helleborus niger *along the stream in early March.*

later, *Anemone blanda* and *A. apennina*, all competing happily with the native wildflowers and pushing through an evergreen ground cover of myrtle (*Vinca minor*).

Gradually my knowledge of gardening and of shade-tolerant plants increased. One of my greatest discoveries was to find the hellebores and to learn how to use them. We now have the Lenten rose (*Helleborus orientalis*) in all its varying shades, as ground cover under shrubs and in our bed of Martagon lilies. It was exciting to discover how easily hellebores grow from seed. Now the plantings of bulbs and vinca on the front slope are acquiring the added dimension of *Helleborus orientalis*, giving a new period of early bloom. True, it will take years to develop, and hundreds of plants, but what a joy a new project can be. The Christmas rose, *Helleborus niger*, is another matter. It does not divide too happily and sets few seeds, so originally we enjoyed it near the house during its blooming time of November and December. Then a happy accident occurred: I acquired a clone of this lovely hellebore which blooms in early spring and sets seed abundantly. I was off! We now produce dozens of new plants and hellebore time in March is a never-ending thrill.

The drop from the back of the house to the sycamore lawn is much steeper than the front slope. It is about twenty feet high and two hundred feet long, and to our inexperienced eyes it seemed a perfect place for a rock garden. After the arrival of tons of rock and endless poring over books, the garden began to take shape. Then came years of trying to make alpines enjoy our hot summers, northern exposure, and deep shade. Finally, we accepted the fact that a rock garden requires much expert attention, and that this was not our most successful adventure. We kept the plants that were happy there, the many kinds of epimediums and lamiums with their attractive leaves; primroses and species tulips for spring color; and varieties of ferny-leaved corydalis, especially the lavender *C. bulbosa*, and *C. lutea*,

which keeps on producing its delicate yellow flowers for months. By the end of May we let the ferns take over — ostrich, beech, bulbous, painted Japanese and great clumps of maidenhair. For the rest of the summer, the garden is a symphony in shades of green and varying leaf forms, until September when the hardy *Begonia evansia* bursts into bloom.

Because the tall sycamores offer high shade, the lawn at the foot of the slope stays lovely throughout the summer and the border beside the stream holds much interest from early spring to fall. In March, *Adonis vernalis* and *A. amurensis,* old-fashioned hyacinths, smaller varieties of daffodils, our special hellebore, and large colonies of white, pink, and rose primulas (*P. sieboldii*) hold sway. This border also has a collection of hostas of varying forms and sizes, among them the great gray *H. sieboldiana,* the stately *H. krossa regal,* the puckered blue *H. tokudama,* and the inch-high *H. venusta.* In July and August great drifts of rosy *Lycoris squamigera* give color to the deep green of summer. In early September, almost overnight, colchicums come up in drifts in the beds. A few weeks later, the fall blooming *Crocus speciosus* appears, a welcome reminder of the spring that will come in a few months.

Alpines are a challenge but so tempting that a small wall now borders one side of our drive and forms a delightful place to grow many miniature daffodils and iris, such as *Iris danfordiae* and *I. azurea.* Here campanulas, dianthus, the lovely double arabis, even some of the drabas, dryas, and saxifrages find a congenial home; it is an easy place for an old gardener to work. The lawn slopes up to a border of tall summer phlox in many colors with a long period of bloom. This area is our one sunny place, given over to a rather nondescript rose garden of hybrid teas with a backdrop of old roses. The rose garden's period of real charm, though, is from the first of April to the first week of June, when it becomes a

Looking from the front lawn across the creek toward a Spiraea prunifolia *blooming along the drive. Yellow* Tulipa niphetos *line one bank.*

Persian carpet of pansies. By early June, the pansies have gottten leggy and have dropped a quantity of seed so we pull them up, mulch the beds heavily, and allow the roses to take over for the rest of the summer. In September, seedling pansies cover the bed, blooming sporadically through October and November, and providing us with flowers for the table until Thanksgiving. Having wintered under a heavy mulch, our Persian carpet reappears again the following spring. Would that the roses were as trustworthy and as easy to manage.

At one time, the small garden behind the house, dominated by two large beech trees, was a boxwood garden with accents of tulips in the spring, white phlox in the summer, and Japanese anemones in the autumn. Dayton is on the northern edge of boxwood hardiness, and during the winters of 1977 and 1978, when the temperature plunged to twenty below zero, we lost most of the box. We renovated the garden, substituting Korean box and yew, but it was not the same. So last year, we turned back the clock and once again have a boxwood garden in the making. Since we are using small plants that have seeded themselves over the years, we anticipate that they will be hardy enough to withstand winters like those of the late seventies.

As the little stream loops around the back of the garden it creates spots for our native spring-flowering *Delphinium tricorne* and the cool summer blooms of astilbes and the native double hydrangea. Some of the water from the stream is diverted to fill a swimming pool, which is planted right to the edge so that it resembles a woodland pond.

Always our plan has been to have the gardens blend into the woodland, to keep the illusion of indistinct boundaries between garden and woods, and to use native vegetation, with species rather than cultivars. Although we have succeeded in having bloom from late February, when the aconites and the witch hazels open, until December, when the last of our Christmas roses fade, the flowers take second place to the beauty and serenity of the woodland setting.

About six years ago I gave the gardens and the woodland to the Montgomery-Dayton Park Board, with an endowment for upkeep and a contract that the gardens be kept in their present form in perpetuity. I have the privilege of living here for my lifetime.

Young box curving around the back lawn. Trilliums and snowdrops circle the beech. Redbud trees in the distance are a haze of pink.

Ann Leighton

LITTLE HILL, IPSWICH, MASSACHUSETTS

A chance peony seedling saved by Ann Leighton and named for her daughter Emily.

GARDENING IN A COUNTRY where the landscape is likely to be wild, jealously beautiful, and possibly stretching for miles, any gardener will do well to fall in line at the start. When we first moved to our "little hill" with its Dutch-gabled summer cottage, we knew we must abandon the elegant small formal garden designed for the former owner by Arthur Shurcliff (later known for re-creating the gardens of Williamsburg). The house perched on the edge of an old gravel pit, the land fell away thirty feet to sea level, and our property of twenty acres included ten of salt marsh on one side and two under the fresh water of a "made" pond on the other. The only view that was not to the horizon was toward a larger hill to the north. Southward the eye was constantly lifted to blue hills across wide marshes and a tidal river. On the east were white dunes and bits of blue sea seen across the fields. Sunsets dyed the pond to the west through limbs of large trees. In learning to garden within this view I knew that interruption of its full sweep would make the open spaces toward the horizon more arresting. The Japanese encouraged me long ago to stand backwards to a spectacular view and look at it upside down between my knees, so I know that concentration between boundaries enhances any view. I therefore concentrated on three or four openings through blocks of trees to establish varied views across marshes and the seaside boundaries of dunes and hills.

My husband, who had gardened all about the world and was a fancier of exotic plants, insisted on growing everything from seed. He hacked into the middle of the wild brush-covered slope of the northern part of the property and made a natural-seeming bank of rock garden plants that extended from the back of the house to where it tapers off to meet my newly established perennial border at the northeast corner of the lawn. My border started with two wide beds in front of the house behind a terrace that my husband covered with flagstones. The border crosses the four-foot drop to lawn level to run along the south side of the lawn and curve east at an old stone boundary wall and run up the hill against the wall. At the top of the hill where the horizon rides above the flowers, the border retires into a grouping of old shrub roses and a grove of flowering trees. This comprises what might be called the garden proper, if it ever looked to be such.

Behind the house on the entrance side, a grove of evergreens planted en masse

A mille-fleurs tapestry in the rock garden — pink, white and lavender perennial geraniums interplanted with yellow potentilla, blue veronica, and gray-leaved Cerastium tomentosum.

years ago, later thinned out by a hurricane, shelters azaleas and rhododendrons. This leads across the road to the "woodlot" beside the pond. Here I have my wildflowers in a valley, a deciduous wood of daffodils, and a skein of paths, one leading along the shore for glimpses of the pink and white water lilies and blue pickerel weed in the pond.

Lying before the house, the vegetable garden is hidden by the bank of low-growing evergreens below the terrace. Below and beyond it, a mown path around a large field bordered by flowering trees and shrubs brings the walker up the slope and back into the garden.

While my husband grew whatever he wished for from seed, I relied upon plundering. On fishing trips through rural Maine I dug up wild flowers and ferns and begged old ladies for bits and pieces from their brilliantly pretty gardens. Though now a very old lady myself, I still refer to their gifts with fresh gratitude, sometimes to the surprise of today's visitors.

But a garden is like a party — more fun if you know the histories of the guests as well as both their familiar and formal names. My *Hosta grandiflora,* for instance, I have had all my life. I brought it from the garden of my childhood in Portsmouth, New Hampshire, which was divided into an eighteenth-century "backyard garden" in three sections, each behind the other, of flowers, fruits, and vegetables. A formal nineteenth-century "front garden" had gigantic ornamental trees, a raised center bed for tulips (changed for the summer into cannas surrounded by coleus), and four cut-out beds, two of laburnums underplanted with this handsomest of all hostas. Old Japanese quinces were in the other two cut-out beds, and a wisteria climbed three stories to the balustraded roof.

From this old garden I brought also the monkshood, *Aconitum napellus,* the little early-blooming *Corydalis bulbosa,* and the *Polemonium reptans,* given me as a child by the first of my kindly old ladies under its pre-Linnaean name of "blue Greek valerian." She assured me it would withstand being transplanted in full bloom, as it had been chosen to hide the hasty burial of the family silver during the War of 1812 when it was feared the British were coming into Portland harbor. My old reliables — lungwort (*Pulmonaria officinalis*), with pastel spring flowers and lovely gray-spotted leaves; cushion spurge (*Euphorbia epithymoides*), providing pretty pale gold mounds of early color; yellow circleflower (*Lysimachia punctata*) of midsummer; and *Lysimachia clethroides,* the gooseneck variety that offers white flowers through the late summer — were all plucked from farm flower beds. So were many of my roses, like Father Hugo's rose with golden sprays in late spring, *Rosa rubrifolia* with delicate pink flowers set amid lovely blue-gray foliage, and the eglantine with its sweetly scented leaves, plus those nearly unidentifiable shrub roses dug from the fields and dooryards of the early settlers. My special joys after the little species crocuses have bloomed in clouds on the upwards slope of the

Looking south from the rock garden across the border to the salt marsh beyond. The steps lead down to the lawn from the flagstone terrace.

lawn are the peonies and iris in the border. I grow all kinds of peonies and save the seedlings, both herbaceous and tree, occasionally with charming results. Deer do not eat peonies or iris. The wide wild view exacts no penalties from them.

As my border stands free except for a gray running-rail fence and a stone wall, its background is often the sky. I have found that tall plants of almost any color tend to disappear against the blue horizon. One that doesn't is *Macleaya cordata,* the plumed poppy found on the Chinese mainland by the McCartney mission in the late eighteenth century. It will also secure any slope, a necessity when gardening on a rise or fall where imposing bulwarks are needed to keep one from feeling one is falling down the slope with the flowers. As for color, shades of bright pink are distracting, perhaps because there seems no natural toning with the greens and golds of the marshes. White seems to stand out unnaturally. Most satisfactory is a border of lemon, saffron, and blues, with touches of scarlet like those touches of lacquer red that Chinnery flicks into his portraits.

Gardening on a slope has some great advantages. The commonest Japanese maple is better seen from below, its leaves given extra beauty when viewed against the sun. A weeping forsythia trails to great advantage down a ten-foot stone wall above the steps. Walking upwards through a drift of naturalized jonquils is dazzling if the planting widens out as one ascends. A plot of lowly bunchberry (*Cornus canadensis*) is lovely if come upon suddenly below its cousins, the American and Korean dogwood trees.

While one's home garden may be one's true love, I have a deep attachment to that of the 1640 Whipple House in Ipswich. Here I maintain a seventeenth-century garden designed by Arthur Shurcliff in 1950. He laid it out and I located, found and planted material for which I have discovered written, local, seventeenth-century evidence culled from measles-cures, from inventories, from letters, from travelers' accounts. It is a brightly pretty, rather crammed small garden (which is open to the public seven months of the year). I also love the nearby collection of old shrub roses, chiefly gifts from those who first rescued them from cellar holes. I have planted them in a large horseshoe in double rows, to curve out on either side of a garden seat. Blooming only once a year, their fragrance is unforgettable throughout the rest of the season, their individual characters and colors the delight of their brief festival in early June.

And so one goes on enjoying gardening, especially at home even after twenty years of gardening alone. A garden continues to be a joy when other joys have departed, even when there is no garden visible to other eyes and one's flower beds and shrubberies are under snow; then my garden exists in mind only. Sometimes sheets of snow cover parts well into March. Snowdrops acquire an added luster surrounded by their implied glory. As George Washington commented during his tour of the thirteen states, the "quality" of New England agriculture, "considering it is under snow for five months of the year," can be ascribed only to "the industry of its inhabitants."

A sweet cherry tree, 'Blackheart', marks the corner where the rock garden slopes down to meet the perennial border.

THE GARDEN OF

Mary Frank

WOODSTOCK, NEW YORK

Looking toward the house in June.

Looking toward the mountain laurel hedges in July, when daylilies and phlox surround the sculpture.

THIS PLACE is a small patchwork house that was probably originally a hunters' cabin and last belonged to a painter. It is set in five and a half acres of northeastern woodland, which also contains a creek beside the road and a creekbed at the base of a great hill that goes for miles to Tannersville. When I got the house ten years ago it seemed to have no garden, just the dark presence of great pines, maples, and birches — black and white. They were majestic but hovering.

The first task was to clear endlessly and establish paths, up the hill, meandering to the creek and to the great boulder behind the studio. Then we formed enclosures surrounded by the native laurel (*Kalmia latifolia*), which grows lushly everywhere. Later Barry Benepe and I created an arcaded allée over an old woodland path climbing the hill by bending and tying witch hazel across it. We had made an arching bower of changing colors for all the seasons.

I've never really come to terms with the climate, especially its late springs and early frosts. Even in the summer there are lots of cold nights. Then there is the challenge of the clay soil, which is really only a thin layer over the rocks below. It's like doing dental work on a dinosaur to dig even a little planting hole.

As more space was cleared, I brought in many wildflowers, like bluebells, New York asters, columbine, foxgloves, daylilies and cinnamon ferns. I also used the tansy and coneflowers that are in a boat-shaped central bed in front of the house. Over the years I've added spring bulbs and hardy perennials, like iris and balloon flowers. The hay fern has filled in everywhere. I let some of it stay, because while I do like bringing plants and trees in and setting them where I choose, I also love the chance element of what naturally comes back in variations with each season.

In planting the flowers I try for both continuity and surprise. One of my greatest pleasures was in having a hummingbird come to drink from a bouquet I had just picked and held in my hand, and then to fly over to drink from a nearby honeysuckle.

I put my sculptures about in the garden, out on the stumps of trees cut down and on rocks. Sometimes I put the smallest works in the niches of huge boulders. The changes of season and growth alter the pieces, sometimes even burying them with foliage and flower. It's a pleasure to see them in changing light and changing

A few annuals set like jewels around the ubiquitous rocks.

weather, particularly in the rain, because the color becomes so strong. It's an experience you can't have in even the most wonderful gallery or museum.

For me a garden is a living, breathing creature. It is always a mysterious joy to see color come up out of the cold earth in early spring. Flowers have given me so much for my work. Every year I find one more thing that I've planted becomes content for it. It's a little bit like having a new character in a play. I tend to draw one flower at a time, although I have been doing drawings, prints and sculptures of nasturtiums for at least fifteen years. I have always drawn them and learned about color from them, how it can be deeply opaque or sheerly translucent, lush and soft or blazing and celestial.

And I find there is a great community in gardening. I am very much aware of how people everywhere have gardened, on rooftops or in deserts, planting in pots or growing roses in old olive oil tins. I've always thought a roadside garden is like a gift for everyone passing by. I don't have one, as the creek separates me from the road. But my friends share in my garden with divisions of harebells and foxgloves and other generous growers. One friend sent me columbine seeds from the Himalayas, and the flowers are wonderful, but not more wonderful than the

Golden foliage of the witch hazel lights the arcade in early October.

COUNTRY GARDENS

native jewels. I read old herbals and imagine the beauty of the wildlings they describe. The velvety grace of the great mullein I know. Here it is considered an awful weed but it is much appreciated in English gardens. An "ordinary" zucchini in full bloom, catching the early morning light, seems as elegant as anything I know.

I don't think one can own this land — it seems ridiculous, like owning water or air. But one can care for it and transform it, always aware of how quickly it returns to its previous state if unattended. A garden, as everyone knows, is an attempt at paradise, and when friends come and we sit or walk in mine, it does feel like one.

The boulder provides a base for the large sculpture and niches for a group of miniatures that bask in the early winter sun.

Senecio aureus *studs the lawn each May and then disappears for the rest of the year.*

*A spring medley of white scilla, forget-me-nots (*Myosotis semperflorens)*, and* Phlox divaricata *carpet a slope and border a fence under the shelter of a hawthorn tree. Clumps of* Macleaya, *Siberian iris, yarrow, and* Campanula trachelium *will take over for the summer show.*

Joanna Reed

LONGVIEW FARM, MALVERN, PENNSYLVANIA

MY FIRST EXPERIENCE as a gardener was as a somewhat reluctant apprentice to a newly acquired father-in-law. He made the plans for our joint efforts and vegetables were our goal. But his advice and assistance came on weekends and our most successful crop the first year was fieldstones. Soon wartime gasoline rationing prevented even his weekend trips to the garden and I was left more on my own. Happily I strayed into the wonderful world of ornamental plants, woody and herbaceous.

My first efforts with ornamentals took place behind the garage — a spot chosen because it was out of sight of the house. I built a retaining wall and filled beds above and within it with perennials. A bench was the architectural feature. A mass of lavender planted on the edge of the wall was a fragrant treat for anyone seated there, and a hawthorn tree framed the view of meadow and woods beyond. Now the hawthorn has grown and the sun-loving lavender is faltering in its shade. Gardening is constant change and learning.

I continued to experiment and explore the succession of seasonal changes in my out-of-sight garden. The February bloom of Chinese witch hazel (*Hamamelis mollis*) and the earliest crocus (*C. tomasinianus*) announce that spring is at hand. A little later clumps of white scilla highlight the blues of *Phlox divaricata*, forget-me-nots and amsonia. Sturdy perennials follow in succession: peonies, campanulas, evening primroses, tall daisylike heliopsis and heleniums, globe thistles and sedums. The bright gold stars of *Chrysogonum virginianum* and the soft silver of lamb's ears edge the curving borders. Unless we are plagued with an unusually dry summer, the vivid blue flowers of monkshood and the showy yellow foliage of amsonia provide the late October finale.

Crushed-brick steps leading up a short slope link this border to the pool garden above. Here are a series of delicate delights. The ripening foliage of small daffodils, species tulips, and other early spring bulbs is hidden by windflowers (*Pulsatilla vulgaris*). Trailing soapwort (*Saponaria ocymoides*) and rockroses (*Helianthemum* spp.) spill over the steps a little later. Thymes, sempervivums, geraniums and verbenas of summer are followed by the rich blue of leadwort (*Cerastostigma plumbaginoides*), the starry white of *Allium tuberosum* and the apricot of an August daylily.

August bloomers in the same part of the garden as shown on the preceding page are Helenium *'Copper Spray', echinops, Russian sage (*Perovskia atriplicifolia*) and* Allium tuberosum.

The pool in earlier life was a cistern that collected water from the barn roof for the animals in the yard below. Only seven feet in diameter, it is filled with water lilies and frogs that are a constant delight. A reblooming German iris, 'Sangreal', loves this spot. It flowers first in early May, and again in late November, well after Indian summer. An *Idesia polycarpa,* a star of my garden, stands sentinel at the pool garden entrance. This tree is gloriously festooned through the fall and winter with long panicles of bright red fruits, a veritable garden Cinderella after its nondescript spring and summer green.

In those early days of experiment I built the ever-ready crop of fieldstones into walls, high and low, freestanding and retaining. These were the bones of the garden and created the housing for the plants. Being of a philosophical nature, my husband took pleasure in what he called my "annual checker game." I was continually reshuffling my initial investment of a few plants. My mistakes were legion, but I was learning. Books were a great source of information and inspiration, full of intoxicating prospects. Biographies and journals of great plantsmen and explorers infected me with their enthusiasm. Because of their tenacity and foresight, wildlings from the world over grace our gardens today. In my own fashion, I too became a collector. I accepted offerings from friends, and asked for others. My husband learned to carry a trowel and plastic bags in the car so we could bring home plants and seeds from the wild. A longtime neighbor regularly asked me why I grew "those weeds." But the farmer who raised crops on my neighbor's land and who was the true guardian of his meticulously maintained acres brought me native viburnums, wild crabapples with especially attractive fruit, and other treasures. The Royal Horticultural Society seed list is to me as Christmas is to a child, with its tantalizing choices from over a thousand possibilities. Even the one seed that germinates and matures can be parlayed into drifts through

divisions and cuttings. Early on I learned to share these acquisitions, so if I lost a plant I could ask for a new start in return.

It is in the broad open sweep of space from the back of the house to the woods beyond that many of my most interesting plants flourish. My earlier efforts taught me that a succession of bloom requires space. Here at last was a sun-drenched area to fill with flowers and fragrance. Next to the house is a simple parterre terrace defined by the grays of lavender and lamb's ears. Creeping thymes edge beds filled with wallflowers, wall valerian, pinks, Jerusalem sage, catmint, blackberry lilies and many others. The view from the terrace toward the woods is framed by large island beds planted with shrubs, perennials and annuals. They were originally devised as a protective measure to keep young trees and shrubs safe from the jaws of mowing machines, on the old theory of "safety in numbers" — especially if the numbers are easily recognized as "garden flowers." These beds are mixes of native and exotic plants for continuity of color from flower, foliage, fruit and seed pods. *Senecio aureus,* given to me from a friend's garden, refused to grow in bed or border, but now star-studs the entire lawn each May and then disappears for the next eleven months. As I acquire it, I use more and more native material to cope with the clay soil that is heavy and wet during the winter but by August can turn overnight into parched, cracked hardpan. Now astilbes and daylilies draw attention to the more discreet wet-meadow wild flowers I am encouraging. Lysimachias and lobelias do well in midsummer. White, blue, and violet asters sparkle in the company of red ludwigia foliage and yellow-green lobelia leaves. My first ludwigia, which I found as a barebranched stem covered with boxlike seedpods, was probably bird sown. In time I learned it was *Ludwigia alternifolia.* Despite its almost microscopic seed, it has spread beautifully. Only a rare visitor is familiar with the plant.

Above: Seasonal plantings on the steps leading to the lily pond: German iris and hardy geranium in late May; butterfly weed and allium in July; and leadwort in August.

Top left: The lily pond was once a barnyard cistern.

Centaurea montana, Phlox divaricata, *and* Pulmonaria officinalis *in bloom above parterre beds colored with rosy pink* Lunaria annua *and yellow and orange wallflowers.*

Some plants like eupatoriums, lunaria, and sweet rocket come readily from seed. Others such as the eastern *Penstemon digitalis* and the great blue lobelia (*L. syphalitica*) must be nursery grown and then transplanted into prepared beds. The so-called wild patches need some summer care. I cull unwanted weeds, grasses, and rapacious volunteers before they set seed, mulching the desired plants with the rejects. At the same time I cut back the tall late-blooming asters, goldenrods, and ironweeds to make them stronger and fuller for the fall show while allowing the summer bloomers center stage. In the fall I have to cut back all the herbaceous material since otherwise voles and rabbits nest in the iris and hemerocallis foliage, comfy and warm atop a larder of succulent tubers.

I have also started trees and shrubs from seed when plants are unavailable. Our native buttonbush (*Cephalanthus occidentalis*) is extolled in books for its fragrant balls of white flowers, glossy foliage, fine fall coloring, and attractive seed heads, but is not to be found in commerce. I was allowed to take seed at an arboretum. When I set out the resulting plants three years later, they were immediately devoured by rabbits. The next time I used wire cages to protect the irresistible foliage until the plants reached three feet. Now the rabbits spurn the seedlings that are beginning to come. Almost every plant carries a story of its discovery, linking me in a small way to the "greats" who have so enriched my life.

I am continually increasing the size of these plantings, massing the different varieties so the color and texture carry from a distance. The plume poppy (*Macleaya cordata*) is a beautiful sight, with bold leaves and delicate blossoms. Equally wonderful are its diamond-shaped, mauve-colored seedpods. *Cassia marilandica*, with bright yellow flower spikes, is a good companion plant.

The paths through these plantings bring the garden visitor under the arching branches of an old shagbark hickory and into the woods. Here the ferns have spread into sheets of green fronds with patches of tall cinnamon and royal ferns on either side of a spring-fed rill. *Rhododendron maximum* and *Leucothoe catesbaei*, which I planted when young, now provide masses of evergreen color and interest. Gradually my epimediums, bergenias, shortias, hellebores and cyclamen are spreading and taking their places in harmony with the natives, mayapple, Solomon's seal and patches of ginger.

The old cart road through the woods leads back to the vegetable garden, completing the circuit. Once the cornerstone of my garden-making, the vegetable garden now serves principally as nursery and propagation beds. However, a double border of herbs on either side of the main path will always be kept. On the hottest summer day I enjoy working among the pungent, tasty plants. Varieties of thymes, salvias, basils, oreganos and alliums provide the backbone. A scotch thistle, *Onopordum acanthifolium*, at its best when a great silver rosette, is used as an accent, along with clumps of fennel and dill, rue, clary sage, and two showy milkweeds, *Asclepias tuberosa* and *A. incarnata*. In the background are mountain mints (*Pycranthemum moticum*); these are wondrous shrubby plants, square-stemmed, pungent, more minty than mint, disease- and insect-free, but rarely mentioned in books. They are a nice addition to bouquets, fresh or dried.

This garden, of several acres, is very much a country garden. The small formal

Panicles of bright red berries festoon the bare branches of Idesia polycarpa.

areas and the fringes and woods are integral parts of the whole. My vision is to have the various elements flow together, the mélange of native and introduced plants enhancing one another. In all honesty, I suppose my vision is also a mélange of others' ideas. One author, Doretta Klaber, has written that she hoped that by finding the ideal spot for most of her plants, her weeds would eventually be the seedlings of her favorite flowers. I saw her garden shortly before she died. It was what she envisioned, a Persian carpet of volunteer plants interspersed with those she had long nurtured. I adapted her approach and find that it has helped my garden survive unavoidable periods of neglect. Naturally "evil material" also prospers. How thankful I am that some authors have written of the exhilaration of conquering goutweed and bindweed!

Over the years and through the seasons, the garden has been shared with many visitors. The generosity of gardeners who have shared special plants, and the inspiration of writers who have shared knowledge and experience have kept me cheerfully weeding in summer heat and pruning in winter chill.

Notes of an American Garden Traveler

ELLEN SAMUELS

THE RED BOOKS that Humphrey Repton prepared for potential clients contained a superb promotional gimmick: the various aspects of the country seat were pictured in their unimproved, "before" condition. Overlays then converted the illustration into a perfected vision of Reptonian redesign. Gardeners do this kind of visual trick all the time. They look at the garden as it is and see it as it will be next week, next month, and next year. They even see it as it will be in three years' time, given halcyon weather, successful plant hunting, and good behavior by all the local wildlife, especially the deer.

We draw on many sources to create these mental magic-lantern shows. Nursery and seed catalogues, often the first garden literature the novice encounters, are an unfailing aid to fantasy. But visits to other gardens provide a panorama of more realistic possibilities. We may find that the strawberry begonia we know as a houseplant is hardy enough to mass as a frothy pink-flowering perennial, or that astilbes are the perfect plants to mask the gawky lower branches of tree peonies. Returning to our own garden, we may imagine the darkest corner lit with the bright green and-white foliage of variegated hydrangeas.

In the early stages of my gardening life most of my horticultural visions were drawn from images of English gardens. Awareness of the more practical inspiration to be drawn from American gardens came very gradually.

By good fortune this gardenmaking began in the precincts of Salutation, one of the oldest private landscapes on the North Shore of Long Island. Here Charles A. Dana had commissioned Frederick Law Olmsted to create the plantings on his country estate. Publisher of the New York *Sun*, Dana was one of the original Central Park commissioners and a longtime friend and patron of Olmsted.

When Louise and Junius Morgan replaced the wooden Dana house with a Georgian stone structure in 1929, they added a terrace and an octagonal sunken garden on the south side facing the Olmsted vista. Mrs. Morgan also replanted the eastern extension of the horseshoe path that wraps around the central vista with a double allée of alternately blue and green cedars of Lebanon. For the beginning gardener here was a magnificent gift of mature trees, high yew hedges,

Old roses, delphinium, and lavender produce a flowery extravaganza alongside the swimming pool in Mattie Borden's California garden.

The Olmsted vista at Salutation terminates with a century-old Nordmann fir. The octagonal pool echoes the shape of the classical sunken garden at the south front of the house. Weeping beech flank the semicircular stairs leading to the south lawn. At the right are a quartet of high-pruned copper beeches.

and weathered paving and walls. This was a perfect background for the overlay of flowering plants that I could already imagine tumbling over the walls and lining the paths. So I was off on the first of my gardening expeditions, to the British Isles to see what their gardens would suggest for transforming the vision into reality.

By chance I began in Scotland with the Edinburgh Botanic Gardens, still the most impressive and informative botanic garden I have ever found. Its herbaceous borders are stunning classics of the genre, and nothing could be more helpful than its synoptic gardens — a living dictionary of plants arranged in alphabetical order by family name. After a journey that began in Edinburgh and ended at Sissinghurst, nothing seemed impossible on Long Island.

A great deal was, in fact, impossible, but I would have had many more disappointments without the guidance and generosity of Adele Lovett. Many of the English cottage-garden flowers that I admired were already at home in her gardens. And she had many suggestions for keeping the gardens attractive in all seasons. Adele planted *Kerria japonica* as much for its gleaming green stems in winter as for the yellow flowers of spring. Of course she planted red-stemmed dogwood to glow against a wintry snowbank. Her bulb garden becomes a fern glade so that their fronds will grow up to hide the dying foliage of scillas and trilliums. I was already learning that while we may dream of English gardens, we do better to depend on the reality of our own best examples and on the generosity and experience of our gardening community.

During my first gardening season I called Adele every Monday and asked about her program, and then set up the same one at Salutation. I soon learned that her gardening activities did not include much sitting down. Even on her eight-first birthday when she came to tea with me she did not stay long. She was soon off to refresh her old French roses with their own brew of manure tea. Adele also introduced me to some of the distinguished and distinctive gardens that have flourished for decades on Long Island. The garden of her good friend Bertha Rose not only housed an extensive hosta and perennial collection but also offered a solution to the problem of accommodating a swimming pool in a naturalistic manner. A waterfall, a slate-gray lining, contours developed by experimenting with a garden hose, and a kind of rock-garden planting along one side all eased the pool into the landscape. Mrs. Rose used more formal elements, like hedges, paving, and stairs, than Adele did, but she liked to blur straight lines with cascades of alchemilla, epimediums, ferns, green nicotiana, and other graceful plants.

The nearby Coe estate, now known as Planting Fields Arboretum and administered by New York State, is a showcase of mature trees, including an enormous specimen of the lovely summer-flowering sourwood (*Oxydendron arboreum*). Here is also a synoptic garden of plants suitable for our soil and climate.

Old Westbury Gardens, another old North Shore estate now open to the public, retains the rich variety of herbaceous plants that characterized it as a private garden. Perhaps this atmosphere, so often lost in such transitions, has survived because family members and friends have had so large a role in helping Peggy Phipps Boegner to preserve her mother's gardens. One of Mrs. Boegner's key horticultural advisers was her classmate Natalie Wagner, who had created her own notable garden in Islip, Long Island, and had served as president of the Garden Club of America in the 1960s. Her special project was the re-creation of the miniature gardens that had surrounded the Phipps children's playhouses. The two-acre walled garden is breathtakingly beautiful, with a unique combination of annuals, perennials, and tender plants, some familiar like dahlias, some exotic like the Brazilian *Tibouchina urvilleana* with velvety blue flowers in late summer. Its color scheme is as intricately worked out as any that Gertrude Jekyll devised.

As for my own garden, it was the swimming pool and the perennial borders that offered the first challenge. For the pool I wanted the atmosphere of a sunlit glade, and I composed the plantings almost entirely from the rayed flowers of the daisy family, together with sunny masses of heliopsis, helenium, and rudbeckias. Splashes of gold from the earliest leopard's bane to the last chrysanthemum cheer the swimmer or sunbather from Memorial Day to Columbus Day.

The perennial border began as a conventional collection of iris, peonies, phlox, and the like. But I soon saw that if I wanted real impact I would have to double the width and add more statuesque plants. Adele contributed the tall white aster relative, *Boltonia asteroides*, for the back, metallic blue *Echinops ritro* for the middle, and the delicate, almost ever-blooming yellow *Coreopsis verticillata* for the front. Even with these and other prolific plants there were such large gaps that I began adding shrubs like broom, vitex, buddleia, and polyantha roses. I never suspected until I read Christopher Lloyd years later that I had invented my own version of what he named the "mixed border." And thinking that I was defying the laws of propriety by rarely having a neatly graphed garden plan, I was inordinately pleased when watching Russell Page at work one spring to find that he too planted without a paper plan, ordering myriads of possible plants, arranging them on the spot, sending back the surplus and ordering more if needed.

Splashes of color from the gloriosa daisies and heliopsis brighten Salutation's swimming pool in August.

White-margined hostas massed around the pond and hydrangeas at the far side of the sunken garden at Salutation give surges of color to a setting dominated by the contrasting forms of pyramidal weeping beeches, and the columnar trunks of the cooper beech.

Adele Lovett's bulb garden becomes a fern glade, the fronds hiding the dying foliage of scillas and trilliums.

The next stage of my garden travels was an extended excursion into the gardens of the past, when I began the Cloisters Garden Committee in 1979 at the request of the Metropolitan Museum of Art. The gardens at the Cloisters, which houses a splendid collection of medieval art, have always added to the special beauty of the place and been a kind of supplemental reference collection. But by the late seventies many of the plantings need rejuvenation and refinement. The research for this task led me to England again and to Rosemary Verey at Barnsley House in the Cotswolds. After many visits to Barnsley it is still difficult to choose between the delights of Rosemary's library and of her garden. A founder member of the English Garden History Society, she invited me to spend hours studying herbals in her collection and even more time wandering the garden paths, collecting seeds and cuttings. But not all the plants I was seeking for the Cloisters' collection could still be found within the confines of a cultivated garden. Many of them had been only barely tamed wildlings in medieval gardens and had long ago escaped back into the English countryside. So I had to find English friends who would admit to having such "weeds" around as Herb Robert (*Geranium robertianum*), named for either a saint or a pope and once a valued plant of many external and internal medicinal applications. Butcher's broom, Italian arum, and birthwort came from the Chelsea Physic Garden through the kindness of Allan Patterson, who was then its director. He escorted me through the gardens with trowel and plastic bags at hand. The birthwort (*Aristolochia clematitis*) went into the medicinal bed at the Cloisters next to the motherwort (*Leonurus cardiaca*) that I found as a weed in my own fields. (There is a charming old prescription for motherwort that exhorts you to drink an infusion of it and live to be "the astonishment and grief" of waiting heirs.) *Melilotus officinalis*, with honey-scented white clover blossoms, was another uninvited guest at Salutation that traveled to the Cloisters. The gardens at the Cloisters flourish through the care of staff horticulturists, and the continuing support of the Garden Committee.

All this is not ancient history. The medieval mix of ornament and utility in a confined space also suits our time. The small urban garden is our equivalent of the *hortus conclusis* in a hostile world. Natives of the medieval woodlands adapt well to shady city yards, and I have enjoyed placing flowers with names like heart's ease, honesty, and dame's rocket in city gardens. Basil, lemon balm, and mint lend fragrance to these retreats and flavor to the kitchen. Medieval vegetable gardens were particularly attractive because violets and roses were culinary plants. We are beginning to find our own kinds of ornamental vegetable designs, as evidenced in Rosemary's version at Barnsley (page 181).

When Rosemary and I began talking about this book I knew it would give me an opportunity to explore the contemporary American garden scene as widely as I had researched the gardens of the European past. This was an intimidating undertaking. The sheer size of the country makes it difficult to assess the state of American gardening. But we also lack national periodicals like *Country Life* and the journal of the Royal Horticultural Society that have a long history of informed writing about private gardens. And there is no equivalent to those volumes that appear annually in England describing hundreds of gardens and the days that they

are open to the public. Our closest equivalents come from the Garden Clubs of Virginia and Maryland, which publish excellent booklets that describe all the public and private gardens in those states open during their annual spring garden weeks.

I was determined, however, to try to indicate the artistry of the American gardens and to introduce a few of the dynamic women who imprint our landscape with their personal flair and determination. Since this volume could not be encyclopedic I sought examples of gardens that would demonstrate the wide range of skills and interests that American women bring to their gardens. I also wanted to indicate how they draw on differing talents and resources to create gardens in a variety of sites and climates. That meant there is room in the book for only one great boxwood garden, and only a few examples of the increasing number of gardens designed around regional native plants. And as spring gardens of dogwoods and azaleas are most familiar, I began looking for gardens that thrive in August and even in October.

It soon became clear that one national characteristic is a cheerful propensity for incorporating the styles of many eras and regions into a single landscape. And when communities of gardeners who enjoy experimenting with design and with plant material come together, the stage is set for some extraordinary gardens. I found this happening now in the Pacific northwest. Such a community was active for more than fifty years in Louisiana. Longue Vue, in New Orleans, the garden of a leader of this memorable group, helps to record the accomplishments of these women who shared horticultural enthusiasm and ideas.

Edith Stern, the chatelaine of Longue Vue (which has been preserved by a private foundation), worked with the landscape designer Ellen Shipman through the 1940s to make a romantic English landscape that included a flower-filled portico garden, an intricate walled kitchen garden, and an elaborately planted south vista that terminated in a reflecting pool before a classical tempietto. Mrs. Stern cared enough about her new gardens to tear down her original house and build a new one with a better garden front. But by 1965, she had become concerned with simplifying the maintenance at Longue Vue. So she traveled to Spain to study Moorish gardens accompanied by her architect, William Platt, the son of Charles Platt who designed the Merrill house and garden in Seattle. They returned to New Orleans to incorporate Andalusian-style waterworks, patterned paving, and container plants into the design at Longue Vue. The new approach fitted quite well into Shipman's original layout — the tempietto was replaced by a Spanish loggia and the reflecting pool was extended into a canal and equipped with jets of water. Walks were paved with pebbled mosaics and fountains; and water channels, pools, and cascades installed throughout.

As great as was her interest in European gardening traditions, Mrs. Stern was also close to a group of women who were deeply involved in preserving and propagating native Louisiana plants. Caroline Dormon, who published two books on Louisiana wildflowers illustrated with her own watercolors, is the best known of the group. She helped Ellen Shipman create the Wild Garden at Longue Vue, with Louisiana iris and wildflowers among native trees and shrubs. The Dormon garden, Briarwood, in Saline, Louisiana, is still well maintained, and efforts are under way to safeguard its collection of native plants.

Mrs. U. B. Evans, who still lives and gardens at Haphazard Plantation in Feriday, Louisiana, across the Mississippi from Natchez, was another member of this garden community. Her particular interest has been horticultural research and training. Jo Evans, despite living on a rural plantation without a telephone or an automobile for most of her married life, was responsible for much collection and propagation of plant materials from old gardens, for the formation of the Louisiana Society for Horticultural Research, and for the establishment of departments of

The south vista at Longue Vue, with the geometric box beds enclosing tree roses, leads to the canal and loggia inspired by the Alhambra.

horticulture in the state university system. In 1954, she decided that Ira S. Nelson, a professor of horticulture and the research director for the Society, needed a challenge, so she raised $100 each from ten friends to send him to Central America to collect amaryllis species. A significant find that has improved amaryllis breeding programs since was named *A. evansae* for her.

Mrs. Evans and her friends were also dedicated to preserving and perpetuating old roses. I had an opportunity when in Natchez with the Southern Garden History Society to roam the cemeteries and back streets with Cleo Barnwell, scouting for treasures. The most interesting finds were in tiny front yards in the poorer sections, not around the mansions. A whole new generation of gardeners now shares this delightful passion for old roses. Mattie Borden in Orinda, California, has done an elegant job of integrating traditional flowers into a contemporary garden. The flowery extravaganza alongside her swimming pool is composed of old roses, delphinium, and lavender for a feast of color and scent.

Not every beginning gardener has the assistance of an Adele Lovett or a Jo Evans. But nearly every essay in this book mentions an older, more experienced gardener who guided the contributor into the horticultural world. Fortunately the growing national interest in gardening coincides with more institutional opportunities for entering the gardening community. Horticultural societies play a significant role, and I have been especially impressed with the example of the Pennsylvania Horticultural Society. With 6,500 members, a mailing list of 130 garden clubs in the region, a headquarters in the historic area of Philadelphia, complete with an appropriate eighteenth-century garden, and an annual budget of $2.5 million, it serves a remarkable mix of inner-city block associations and community gardens, and affluent suburbanites of the Main Line and the estates and country gardens beyond. Members share their gardens with each other through garden-visit programs and through personal journalism in *The Garden Scene*, the bimonthly bulletin of the Society. The Society is perhaps best known for its dazzling annual feat of horticultural showmanship, the Philadelphia Flower Show, which draws a quarter of a million visitors in early March. In recent years visitors have noted the appearance of displays of gardening in the inner city produced by "Philadelphia Green," a program of the Society financed by $500,000 in federal, city, and private funds to promote gardening in the most deteriorated neighborhoods. Their annual city gardens contests have drawn as many as six hundred entries.

New Botanical gardens and arboreta are sprouting across the country, and existing ones are offering more programs for the home gardener. Their plant sales and garden tours are increasingly sophisticated. Educational opportunities at the New York Botanic Gardens have been important to women in the New York metropolitan area for decades. It was there that Helen Morgenthau Fox, whom I quote at the end of this epilogue, received professional training through a self-designed apprentice program. Such a broad range of courses is now regularly available that it is possible to receive a professional certificate in many areas of horticulture, or just to explore an area of personal interest.

When gardeners are looking for ideas for their own properties or are ready to apply the lessons learned in institutional settings, they need to see plants in

Old roses like these in a frontyard in Natchez are sought by members of heritage rose societies to propagate for a new generation of admirers.

Bleeding hearts and 'Crystal' tulips make a delicate and charming picture in Helen Smith's spring garden.

more intimate surroundings. The preservation of personal gardens like Longue Vue or Old Westbury Gardens, so important in itself, also provides visitors with the opportunity to see a variety of domestic landscapes, thus helping to compensate for the absence here of the valuable British custom of opening private gardens to visitors. Not surprisingly, many of the most successful examples of garden preservation have been the work of women who are keen amateur gardeners themselves and know how to encourage the kind of dedicated volunteer assistance that enables the subtleties of personal style to survive in an institutional framework. The Tullie Smith House Restoration in Atlanta is one of the best examples of this process that I discovered in my travels.

Tullie Smith was the last member of her family to live in the plantation-plain-style house they built in the 1840s in De Kalb County, Georgia. After her death the house was moved in 1969 to the grounds of the Atlanta Historical Society. It was the inspiration of Florence Griffin, chairman of the Tullie Smith House Restoration, to enlist the help of expert women gardeners (and it takes one to know one) as volunteers. Since 1972, individual volunteers have planned, planted, and tended each of the gardens around the house that re-create the horticultural environment of the early settlements of inland Georgia. Beyond the house there is a vegetable garden, an abbreviated planting of field crops, a native wildflower collection, and even a hillside spilling over with early escapees from the garden like yarrow, evening primrose, and Scottish harebells. Enjoying the fence flower-yard with its swept earth paths and bright array of old roses, heliotrope, laced pinks, and other period plants, it is easy to imagine the lady of the house, obviously a meticulous and dedicated gardener, stepping out the door to snip blossoms for her potpourri. The garden is as lively as the one in the same tradition at Cedar Lane Farm that Jane Symmes writes about in this book.

Lavenders circle the mixed plantings of purple cabbage, ornamental kale and mint in Rosemary Verey's vegetable garden.

Dogwoods, in Houston, is another garden in this book that has a counterpart open to the interested visitor: neighboring Bayou Bend. These gardens are open on a regular basis by reservation because their creator, Miss Ima Hogg, donated the estate in the mid-sixties to the Houston Museum of Fine Arts as a showcase of American decorative arts. The gardens are an anthology of garden styles, from a naturalistic woodland of native trees to a formal terraced garden with a statue of Diana mirrored in a reflecting pool and backed by tall clipped yew columns. Miss Ima continued to develop the gardens throughout her life at Bayou Bend, from the first enclosed parterre plantings of 1927 to the white woodland plantings of the early sixties that she dedicated to the memory of Wheeler, her gardener of thirty years. The garden called Carla commemorates the hurricane of that name that cleared the space for it. Miss Ima was one of the first to introduce azaleas and camellias to Houston. Until this innovation, garden tours took place in April, when roses are at their peak. But in 1936, with shrubs in bloom at Bayou Bend, at Dogwoods (then owned by Miss Ima's brother Mike), and in the Hansen garden across the street, the River Oaks Garden Club sponsored the first Azalea Trail. The club now provides both volunteer help in the Bayou Bend gardens and financial support, having recently increased its endowment to half a million dollars.

The Chicago Botanic Garden has found a way to preserve a personal garden within its own confines. When I began looking for fine gardens in the suburbs around Chicago I constantly heard, "If you could only have seen Edith Farwell's garden!" Edith Farwell's particular interest was herbs, but design was as important to her as the plants. Although her own garden in Lake Forest is no more, its spirit is preserved in the Farwell Gardens of the Chicago Botanic Garden, which were funded by the Women's Board and the Lake Forest Garden Club. Designed by Board member Janet King Poore, they are an intimate complex of three separate

Margot Parrot has transformed the boulder beside her eighteenth-century house in Manchester, Massachusetts into the site of a choice collection of alpines and other rock garden plants.

herb collections in which she has used plants and design elements most associated with Mrs. Farwell. The centerpiece is a formal enclosed ornamental herb garden sheltered within three living walls of Selkirk crab, while the entry is screened by a pleached row of thornless cockspur hawthorn. Because of the "unruly nature" of culinary herbs, they are in a separate garden with the beds delineated by the wattle fencing that Mrs. Farwell was the first to import to the Midwest. The garden nearest the entry is a collection of scented plants. Here the standard heliotropes, another Farwell device, are grown from cuttings from her own plants.

I have mentioned these examples of garden preservation simply as an incentive to explore similar examples that are becoming increasingly available across the country.

Several of our contributors have written about how the constraints and opportunities provided by location have affected their gardens. However, I found no more dramatic example of creative adaptation to site than in the garden of Margot Parrot in Manchester, Massachusetts. Her early eighteenth-century house is only a few feet from a three-story boulder deposited by those same glaciers that created the stony fields that plague so many American gardeners and have made stone walls a ubiquitous feature of our garden architecture. Mrs. Parrot's approach has been to gradually transform the boulder into a rock garden, whose upper reaches she tends from a ladder. Fortunately she enjoys working with alpine plants, saying that rocks are as much fun to play with as plants.

I had expected to find many women who took pleasure in working with herbaceous plants, but the number who are collecting, hybridizing, and propagating woody material has been a surprise. The best known of them may be Polly Hill. Because of her remarkable ambition, the range of azaleas, camellias, Kousa dogwoods, crabs and magnolias that are available for our gardens has some choice new additions. In 1957, at age fifty, she decided to create an arboretum from seed on her summer place on Martha's Vineyard. And as she says, when you grow plants from seed you have a chance of raising something brand new. Working in a happy collaboration with Dr. Rokujo, an amateur with the largest collection of rhododendrons in Japan who sent her seeds that are crosses of an azalea that spreads like a ground cover, she propagated the azaleas known as the North Tisbury hybrids. Polly Hill has now selected varieties not only in the natural red of their Nakaharai ancestors, but in pastels like 'Pink Pancake' and 'Late Love'. Another azalea now on the market through her efforts is the fragrant evergreen with lavender flowers that she calls 'Ladylocks'. Flowering trees have taken longer to mature, but she has selected some very promising varieties of Korean dogwood, tea crab and *Magnolia macrophylla*.

As I traveled, searching for the gardens that make up the substance of this book, I looked for clues about the importance of gardening to younger women in a period when so many of them are leading nontraditional lives. For Barbara Robinson, who gardens near Litchfield, Connecticut, and Cynthia Woodyard of Portland, Oregon, it is quite clear that gardening is an essential activity, and each has found her own way to immerse herself in it. Barbara only discovered the appeal of gardening after she and her husband bought their weekend property in

Connecticut. She had no childhood horticultural experiences, having grown up on Long Island with "shrubs and hired gardeners." As the first female partner in one of Manhattan's most prestigious law firms and the mother of two boys, she has added work in the garden to her schedule only by severely limiting lounging around on weekends. It is the lure of the plants that has most intrigued her, and the proximity of some well-known nurseries has allowed her to indulge her curiosity. She also takes comfort in the fact that, unlike clients and family, plants don't have identity crises: a violet doesn't suddenly yearn to bear strawberries.

Barbara Robinson has found gardening so irresistible that it has to be included in a life that already includes a demanding career as well as a family. Cynthia Woodyard, in Portland, shows that women are still choosing to concentrate on gardening as a primary interest.

Cynthia says that her earliest gardening activities were a way of avoiding housework; "I spent the first ten years of life with my brothers in the woodlands along our stream building sapling forts and log rafts, and admiring escaped drifts of grape hyacinths. Then my mother gave me the pruners, which not only created better forts, but beautified her borders and rescued me from the vacuum cleaner. Little did she know that later, as a frustrated art student looking for an appropriate tool and medium, I would return to the pruners and the earth. And of course, when dear Aunt Mary gave me her old copy of *Wood and Garden* by Gertrude Jekyll, everything came into focus." For the last nine years, since her marriage and move to an old house in a derelict garden, she has been exploring the gardening world, inspiration often coming from the need to provide settings for new plants. She knows that it is usually possible to put a better idea into reality: for example, "A certain old *Rhododendron loderi* has been trotted around the garden swinging from the middle of a long pole to four different locations, each better than the last."

As Cynthia began to want to garden more expertly, she had the inspiration of writing to Allan Bloom, the English wizard of the perennial garden, to ask if she could work in his garden. To her delight he replied favorably and her weeks at Bressingham were enough to set her off on a continuing redesign of her garden to include more and more interesting perennials. She is increasingly asked to act as a garden consultant and runs a yearly sale of perennial plants she has propagated. Since meeting Faith Mackaness she has become more and more involved in the community of gardeners in Portland, especially the Hardy Plant Society and the Rock Garden Society.

Almost every contributor to this book and indeed almost all the other good gardeners I met expressed in one way or another the feeling that the garden is a canvas for creative expression. In an interview in 1938, Ellen Shipman said it this way: "Until women took up landscaping, gardening in this country was at its lowest ebb. The renaissance of the art was due largely to the fact that women, instead of working over their boards, used plants as if they were painting pictures, as an artist would."

In the American garden palette, delicate pastels in the petals and grays in fleecy gray foliage are still the overwhelming favorites. The delightful interplay of

Cynthia Woodyard uses shrubs and trees in her Portland garden to create "rooms" furnished with island beds and water features.

Carol Ann Mackay mixes the reds and yellows of midseason Darwin tulips for an explosion of spring color beside the door of her Minnesota home.

Deep purple Japanese iris and strong orange Exbury azaleas glitter in the California sunlight in the Montecito garden of Mrs. Brayton Miller.

the shapes and colors of interplanted 'Crystal' tulips and bleeding hearts (*Dicentra spectabilis*) in Helen Smith's spring planting captures the appeal of these pale shades. And I can still conjure up a scene that I composed accidentally by planting leftover blue nepeta and pale pink astilbe beneath the overhang of an arching white azalea.

But after seeing so many gardens composed in the colors of a bag of sugared almonds, I have become "color thirsty," as Louise Beebe Wilder called the symptom in a chapter, "New Color Schemes in the Garden," of *Adventures in a Suburban Garden* (1931). Urging less "aloof refinement," she proposed "contrast as well as harmony, richness and depth and brilliance as well as delicacy and refinement and all used with a light touch and a freedom from rule of thumb. . . ." The riotous assemblage of tulips in Carol Ann Mackay's Minnesota garden shows just such an approach. And the combination of orange and purple that Mrs. Brayton Wilbur uses in her Montecito, California, garden, is all that Louise Wilder could have asked. Mrs. Wilder was even ready to try to rehabilitate magenta, noting that "pure magenta, especially combined with velvety texture, is one of the most lovely of hues and shows itself friendly enough in association with other hues provided the reds and salmon pinks — its inalienable enemies — are kept at a proper distance." She suggested combining it with creams, corn yellow, lavender, silver, cool blue, and pure purple.

We rarely think about the effect of changing light throughout the day on flower color. But I have noticed that a rose like 'Tropicana', which can seem gaudy at midday, takes on an almost magical glow in the flat gray light of early morning or late afternoon. Perhaps we might think of gardens for different times of day as well as different seasons.

Helen Morgenthau Fox, who came to gardening after marriage and while raising children in suburban New York, wrote a number of very useful books — especially *Adventures in My Garden*, which contains an immense amount of practical information about gardening in the area around Peekskill. But a few words that she wrote in an introduction to a book by Louise Beebe Wilder in 1932 sum up my feelings after this garden odyssey.

> Although most amateur gardeners begin tentatively and with gloves on it is pleasant to see how they slowly change until the love for growing plants and arranging them artistically takes complete possession of them and the whole world is colored over with the hue of their hobby. Although they do not go into gardening with the object of improving themselves, yet shy people become friendly and stiff ones thaw out, and the most unsuspected talents for combining colors both indoors and out are manifested, as is the ability for making and recording scientific observations. The further one goes along the road the more branches and related subjects one finds opening off from it and one has no idea whither these little side paths are going to lead. One thing is certain, however, that the people one meets as one travels along the garden path are delightful, remarkably generous and invariably genuine.

The Gardeners

MARTHA WHALEY ADAMS is the daughter of Emily Whaley and the mother of two young children. As Marty Adams she is an artist and photographer and the resident horticultural commentator for WIS-TV South Carolina. The co-author of two local garden guides, she is also the chairman of Columbia Green, Inc., which she recently organized to support downtown gardens.

MARIE STURWOLD AULL was born in Cincinnati and graduated from the University of Cincinnati. After her marriage in 1923, she moved to Dayton and began making her garden. She has always been interested in conservation and served on the boards of the Garden Club of America and the National Audubon Society. She is the donor of the Aullwood Audubon Center and Farm and was instrumental in establishing the Dayton-Montgomery County Park District.

ALICE HAND CALLAWAY, born in 1912, grew up in Pelham, Georgia, and attended Mount Vernon Seminary before her marriage in 1930. While her family and gardening are her greatest interests, she has been active in civic affairs in La Grange and served on the board of the Callaway Foundation for over 25 years.

MEDORA STEEDMAN BASS was born in St. Louis in 1909, the daughter of Carrie Howard and George Fox Steedman. After her marriage to George E. Bass and the birth of her four children, she ran a dairy farm. Volunteer work in family planning prompted her to enroll at forty-two as a freshman at Bryn Mawr College, where she eventually earned a masters degree. She then became a counselor, lecturer, and writer about sex education.

LURLINE ROTH COONAN, born in San Francisco in 1920, is the mother of three married children. Her first exposure to gardens was in growing up at her mother's estate, Filoli. Mrs. Coonan is active in California garden and horticultural organizations and has received the Medal of Merit Award of the Garden Club of America. A noted horsewoman in her youth, she continues to ride regularly, helping with the cow work at the family ranches.

PAMELA CUNNINGHAM COPELAND has always been interested in wildflowers, so it is not surprising her garden should reflect this enthusiasm. Her other activities are concerned with the preservation of our American heritage.

MARY FRANK was born in England but came to New York with her mother in 1940, at the beginning of the war, and grew up in Brooklyn. Her sculpture, drawings, prints, and other works on paper are in the permanent collections of the Whitney Museum, the Museum of Modern Art, the Metropolitan Museum of Art in New York, the Hirshhorn Museum in Washington, D.C., and twenty other public collections. In New York her work is shown at the Zabriskie Gallery.

MAXINE MCDERMOTT HULL is a native Texan who attended the University of Texas. The mother of two and grandmother of five, she is a collector of eighteenth-century French antiques and an avid tennis player.

ANN LEIGHTON is the pen name of Isadore Leighton Luce Smith, who grew up in a 1790s' garden in Portsmouth, New Hampshire, with a doctor father interested in medical history. She has written two books, *Early American Gardens: For "Meate & Medicine"* and *American Gardens in the Eighteenth Century: "for Use or for Delight,"* and recently completed a chapter on the history of American gardening for the *Oxford Companion to Gardens*. She has planted many gardens for historic houses, including the John Whipple House in Ipswich and the Paul Revere House in Boston.

RUTH WHITE LEVITAN grew up in Washington, D.C., where her father was in government and her mother a writer. She had always wanted to be an artist, but parental urging led her to Columbia University Law School, where she met her husband when they were co-editors of the *Law Review*. She says she gladly gave up law for motherhood, moved to Connecticut, and found that creating a garden was the perfect art form for her.

ADELE BROWN LOVETT was born in New York City in 1899 and married Robert Lovett in 1919. Her husband served as assistant Secretary of War for Air for President Franklin Roosevelt and as Under Secretary of State and Secretary of Defense for President Harry Truman. Mrs. Lovett received the Garden Club of America Award of Merit in 1971 for "sharing with others her vast horticultural knowledge and for her artistry with flowers and plant material shown in her spectacular flower arrangements, civic plantings, and her own beautiful garden."

SALLY MCCUNE MACBRIDE was born in Portland, Oregon, and her youth was divided between Portland, San Francisco, and the Far East, with sojourns in England and Europe. Somehow, sooner or later, influences from this background have crept into her garden. A long-time resident of Woodside, California, she has served on the boards of the Strybing Arboretum, the Saratoga Horticultural Foundation, the Friends of Filoli and Filoli Center, and the Garden Club of America. She is a member of the GCA Rare Plant Group.

FAITH PENNEBAKER MACKANESS grew up in New Orleans and Dallas. She studied art at Tulane University, science at the University of Texas at Austin, and botany and ecology at the graduate school of Tulane. In 1940 she married Francis George Mackaness, then a British subject, and followed him to Haiti, where he worked during World War II. The family, which included three young sons, then moved to northwest Oregon. Mrs. Mackaness has represented the Oregon State Federation of Garden Clubs on the Friends of the Columbia River Gorge for thirty years and prompted the establishment of the Oneonta Gorge Botanical Area of the U.S. Forest Service on the historic Columbia River highway.

CAROL ANN MILLER MACKAY is a native Minnesotan. A sculptor who has taught art history at the Walker Art Center and the Minnesota Institute of Arts, she lectures widely about American Indian art, a special interest. Mrs. Mackay has been involved in architectural preservation and has initiated projects to reuse historic properties for arts activities. Her two older children are in college and her younger daughter is a high-school student.

ANN SMALLIDGE MCPHAIL grew up in Boston and moved to Philadelphia after her marriage. She received training in horticultural arts and related subjects at the Barnes Foundation Arboretum. A garden designer and consultant, she has been actively involved with the design and maintenance of the eighteenth-century garden at the Pennsylvania Horticultural Society since 1966. She is also an educator and lecturer at the Philadelphia Museum of Art, specializing in Oriental Art.

ELISABETH CAREY MILLER majored in art at the University of Washington. She has many civic and horticultural interests and was a founder of the Rhododendron Species Foundation, the Northwest Horticultural Society, and the Washington State Roadside Council. A lecturer, writer, and judge for national and local organizations, Mrs. Miller was the horticulturist for Lawrence Halprin's landscaping of Seattle's Freeway Lid Park. She has been honored by the American Horticultural Society, the XI International Botanical Congress and has received two gold medals from the Garden Club of America, the Amy Angell Collier Montague Medal and the Natalie Peters Webster Medal, of which she was the first recipient. She is also a member of the GCA Rare Plant Group.

GEORGIANNA SHERMAN ORSINI, who grew up in New England, is married to an Italian restaurateur. She has lived in Pawling for the last twenty years and is now making a winter garden in Florida. Her poetry has been published by small presses. The piano makes up the last of the triad of her interests.

LORRIE STOEBER OTTO graduated from the University of Wisconsin in 1942 with an arts degree and trained at the Riveredge Nature Center for her activities as a teacher, lecturer, and environmental consultant. She is actively involved with the Nature Conservancy and the Milwaukee Audubon Society, for which she produces cable TV programs. She has two grown children.

ELEANOR PERÉNYI, the daughter of a naval officer, was brought up in naval stations around the world. Her mother is the novelist Grace Zaring Stone. After her marriage to the late Baron Zsigmond Perényi she lived for several years on her husband's estate in Hungary. A writer and magazine editor, widely known as the author of *Green Thoughts*, she has lived in Connecticut for the last thirty years.

JANE KERR PLATT was born in Portland, Oregon, attended Westover School in Connecticut, and then studied at several art schools in this country and abroad. Her father, Peter Kerr, was a noted northwest amateur gardener. Mrs. Platt serves on the boards of the Rae Selling Berry Botanic Garden in Portland and the Rhododendron Species Foundation of Tacoma, Washington. The Garden Club of America awarded her the Mrs. Oakleigh Thorne Medal for Garden Design in 1984. She is a member of the GCA Rare Plant Group.

JOANNA MCQUAIL REED grew up in Pennsylvania and attended art school for two years before marrying and moving to the country, where she soon began painting with flowers instead of pigments. The mother of five children, she studied at the Barnes Arboretum Foundation and has been active in the Pennsylvania Horticultural Society. She served as president of the Herb Society of America.

PEGGY MCGRATH ROCKEFELLER, the wife of David Rockefeller, is a cattle breeder by vocation, gardener by avocation. While on the board of the New York Botanical Garden she organized and raised funds for their series, *Wildflowers of the United States*. Preservation of farmland and the coast of Maine takes up any leftover time.

MAUREEN SANDERS RUETTGERS grew up in Bloomfield Hills, Michigan, and earned a B.S. in education at Wittenberg University in Springfield, Ohio. She is a member of the New England Hosta Society and is librarian for the Herb Society of America. Sales of fresh herbs to local restaurants and of dried creations at an annual craft market help finance her gardening.

HELEN HUNKER SMITH, born in New Mexico in 1912, earned the degree of Doctor of Jurisprudence from the University of Missouri. She moved with her husband to Colorado Springs in 1946 when he set up medical practice there. They have two daughters, both university professors. The Smiths have traveled widely in Central America, Japan, and Europe, and have been around the world twice. Plants frequently come home with them. She is a past president of the local Horticultural Arts Society.

JANE CAMPBELL SYMMES is a native of Atlanta, Georgia. She developed an interest in historic houses and gardens while taking her degree in the history of art at Agnes Scott College. With her late husband, John Cleves Symmes, she founded Cedar Lane Farm. She served on the first Board of Trustees of the Georgia Trust for Historic Preservation. As a board member of the Madison-Morgan Cultural Center, she conceived the 1983 exhibition, *John Abbot in Georgia: The Vision of a Naturalist Artist (1751–ca.1840)*. She has also lectured on the restoration of historic houses and gardens.

EULALIE MERRILL WAGNER is the widow of G. Corydon Wagner, Jr., a member of the second generation of his family to have gardened at Lakewold. She also tends the gardens of her parents at "Merrill House," now maintained by the Seattle Art Museum. The mother of three, grandmother of twelve, and great-grandmother of five, gardening is her hobby, especially rock plants, rhododendrons, and roses. She is a member of the GCA's Rare Plant Group.

SARAH AND VIRGINIA WEATHERLY are retired — respectively — from a cousin's Bridge Construction Company and from administrative work at the University of Kansas City. Their horticultural knowledge was gained from avid reading of gardening books and by osmosis from their mother, who designed the original garden they now love and tend.

EMILY FISHBURNE WHALEY, the child of a country doctor, grew up in the pineland village of Pineopolis, forty miles north of Charleston. She has lived in Charleston for the fifty years following her marriage to Ben Scott Whaley. For many years she helped maintain the gardens at the Nathaniel Russell House, and her garden is frequently open for the benefit of the restoration of the Aiken-Rhett House.

HANNAH WILLETS WISTER is a long time resident of Oldwick, New Jersey, and a member of the Somerset Hills Garden Club. Among her non-horticultural diversions are her grandchildren and her dogs.

Botanical nomenclature throughout is based on Liberty H. Bailey, *Hortus Third: A Concise Dictionary of Plants Grown in the United States and Canada*.

Photograph Credits

Title page: Steve Crawford.

Introduction: Dick Busher, 10; Courtesy Filoli Center, 13; Julie Kierstead, 15; William Andrew, 16; Courtesy Garden Club of America Glass Slide Collection, 17, 18; Ursula Pariser, Courtesy Dumbarton Oaks, 19; Cynthia Mathews, 20.

Bass: Arthur Sylvester, 22, 23, 24; Marina Schinz, 25, 26, 27.

Symmes: T. R. Crown, 28, 32; Steve Crawford, 29, 30; Copyright by Southern Living, Inc., September 1983, used with permission, 31.

Rockefeller: Linn Sage, 33, 34, 36, 38; Alan Ward, 35, 39.

Callaway: Steve Crawford, 40, 41, 42, 43, 44, 45.

Whaley: Marty Adams, 46; Michael McKinley, 47, 48; Thomas F. Gates, 49.

Adams: Thomas F. Gates, 50, 51.

Levitan: Derek Fell, 52, 53, 54, 55, 56.

Perényi: Emerick Bronson, 57, 58, 59, 60.

Weatherly: Beau Pierce, 62, 63, 64, 65.

McPhail: Ann McPhail, 66, 67, 68, 69.

Smith: Guy Burgess, 70, 72, 73.

Copeland: Marina Schinz, 74, 75, 76, 77, 78, 79.

Field: John Pratt, 80, 81, 82, 83.

Hull: Michael Dunne, 85, 86, 87.

Wagner: Cyrus Happy, 88; Dick Busher, 89, 90, 93; William Andrew, 91, 92.

McKay: Carol Ann McKay, 94, 97, 99; Ellen Samuels, 95; Jane McKenna, 96.

Orsini: Marina Schinz, 99, 100, 102, 103, 105.

Mackaness: Dick Busher, 106; William Andrew, 107, 109, 110; Frank Mackaness, 108.

Platt: William Andrew, 112, 113, 114, 116, 117; John Platt, 115.

Ruettgers: Gregory Trevleaven, 118, 119, 121; Maris-Semel, 120.

Otto: Michael McKinley, 122, 123; Lorrie Otto, 124, 125, 126.

Miller: William Andrew, 127, 128, 129, 130, 131.

McBride: George Waters, 132, 133, 134, 136, 137; Alex MacBride, 135.

Coonan: George Waters, 138, 139, 140, 141, 142.

Wister: Molly Adams, 143, 144, 145.

Lovett: Cynthia Mathews, 146, 148, 149, 150, 151; Michael Dunne, 147.

Aull: Thomas F. Gates, 152, 156, 157; Courtesy of Marie Aull, 153, 154, 155.

Leighton: Patti Hall, 158, 159; Dorothy Monnelly, 160; Ann Leighton, 161.

Frank: Jerry L. Thompson, 162, 165; Ralph Gabriner, 163, 164.

Reed: Franziska Reed-Hecht, 167, 169, 171; Laurie A. Black, 166, 170; Edmund Gilchrist, Jr., 168.

Epilogue: George Waters, 172, 185; Nigel Hudson, 174, 181; Michael McKinley, 175, 177, 182; Ellen Samuels, 178, 179; Cynthia Mathews, 176; Guy Burgess, 180; Cynthia Woodyard, 183; Carol Ann McKay, 184.

Designed by Susan Marsh, with Carol Keller
Edited by Betty Childs
Copyedited by Michael Mattil
Production coordination by Nancy Robins
Composition in Galliard by DEKR
Printed in Italy by Sagdos